A word to the readers

We do not know what is happening to us, and this is precisely what is happening to us, not to know what is happening to us
José Ortega y Gasset

Human today has fallen into a terrible fire, which is called Alienation. Self-forgetfulness causes human to give up loving himself and not discover a reason for his existence. When he cannot discover the cause of his own existence, at certain moments he engages in actions that are often unintentionally anti-human. He does not know what action he is taking and he does not know whether this action was right or wrong in a situation where society has led human to depoliticize. He only acts and finds no reason for his actions. With a logic that considers truth dead and completely relativistic, that person will be more likely to justify his actions and will not seek the truth at all, or anything close to the truth. Human will not understand himself until he seeks to discover the closest thing to the truth, and human who does not know his individual identity will have no understanding of collective identity and Otherness. There is a close relationship between identity and truth. Without identity, there is no truth, and where there is no truth, anonymity shows itself.

The way forward for human is to think about the self. By looking at history, by taking refuge in art, by understanding philosophy, by perusing mythology and cultures, human can see his true face in the mirror and visualize another in the mirror.

The aim of Hermes Magazine is to present beauty and glory to its audience in the form of words, and by publishing the different ideas of writers from different countries and cultures, to some extent represent the true nature of human societies. We are very happy that you are the reader of this magazine and you are following us.

YOUR FRIEND,

Mohammad Abedi

Contents

Art History

Other Articles

Poetry

Short Story

PHILOSOPHY

TRUTH AND POLITICS

BY THOMAS POGGE

We are sitting in a car going 30 kilometers per hour. It's a nice day and the road is straight. But the map tells us that we are approaching a densely populated area where we know we'll have to slow down to 20 km/h, maybe less. There are no other roads we might turn onto; we are stuck with the one we're on.

Our car is a bit unusual. It's an automatic, no clutch or gears. It also has no brakes. And it has a strange time delay in the gas pedal so that any fuel we put to work by depressing the pedal reaches the engine gradually, spread out over the next five minutes. How hard the engine is working depends on how far, on average, the gas pedal has been depressed over the five preceding minutes.

Our chauffeur has been driving cautiously at first, depressing the pedal only slightly. But he's become more assertive recently, pressing the accelerator farther down toward the floor. Most of the acceleration this will cause has not yet occurred.

Some of the passengers are getting restive. The densely populated area is now in sight, and it looks like it's a bit below where we are, so the road ahead seems to go downhill. We can also see from the speedometer that the car is speeding up: 33 – 34 – 35 – 36, in ever more rapid succession. We are worried about the lack of brakes and worried about all the fuel that will still reach the engine over the next five minutes. At our speed, five minutes means 3 kilometers. Do we really want to drive in a densely populated area at 45 or 50 km/h without brakes?

For a few painful minutes, the driver ignores the increasingly urgent appeals from the back seat and keeps depressing the accelerator farther. But now we finally have his attention, and he actually turns down the radio to tell us that he fully shares our concerns. Good! He has a great idea, too: let's all vote to agree that our speed in the densely populated area shall be no more than 15 km/h. We are much relieved; and everyone happily votes for the proposal. But the driver's foot stays where it is, pressing the accelerator halfway to the floor. And the speed is 37 now – no, make that 38. A bottle of champagne is circulating to celebrate our unanimous agreement.

I composed this little parable – under the title Paris Road Trip – six years ago, in the immediate aftermath of the COP 21 in Paris, which had ended with much joy and celebration.[1] Governments had officially agreed that we must keep the average global surface temperature of our planet from rising more than 1.5 degrees Celsius above the pre-industrial level.

I did not share the joy. I was convinced that this COP, like the others, would not work. One reason for my skepticism was the absence of any binding agreement on a division of responsibilities toward achieving the task undertaken. States were asked to make whatever commitments they liked and then invited to try to fulfill them. A big invitation to creative accounting, which governments and their COP delegates have been perfecting in subsequent years.

I had seen it all before. At the 1996 World Food Summit in Rome, the 186 participating governments declared: "We pledge our political will and our common and national commitment to achieving food security for all and to an ongoing effort to eradicate hunger in all countries, with an immediate view to reducing the number of undernourished people to half their present level no later than 2015."[2] That Rome Declaration, too, caused widespread celebration. People overlooked the fact that, despite their use of the word "immediate," governments had allowed 19 years for solving even just half of the problem – far longer than any political leader of the day could reasonably expect to remain in office.

The promise to halve world poverty by 2015 was renewed in the UN Millennium Declaration of the year 2000, when the 191 UN member states committed themselves to the goal "to halve, by the year 2015, the proportion of the world's people whose income is less than one dollar a day and the proportion of people who suffer from hunger."[3] Close inspection of the two texts reveals a subtle but important shift. While the earlier Rome Declaration spoke of halving by 2015 the number of undernourished, the later Millennium Declaration speaks of halving by 2015 the proportion of people suffering from hunger and extreme poverty.

Substituting "proportion" for "number" makes a considerable difference. The relevant proportion is a fraction consisting of the number of poor people in the numerator and "the world's people" in the denominator. With world population expected to increase by 2015 to about 120 percent of what it was in 2000, a 40%-reduction in the number of poor to 60% of what it was in 2000 suffices to cut the proportion in half. The Rome Declaration promises a 50% reduction in the number of poor by 2015. The Millennium Declaration promises only a 40% reduction in this number. Clearly, the goal posts had been moved – against the world's poorest and most vulnerable people.

Shortly after its adoption, Article 19 of the Millennium Declaration was re-written at the UN as a set of eight Millennium Development Goals (MDGs), of which the first, MDG#1, once more restates the commitment to halve poverty and hunger by 2015. But here, yet again, the text is diluted through two further revisions. One revision makes MDG#1 track the poor and hungry not as a "proportion of the world's people," but as a proportion of people in the developing countries.[4] This change is significant because the latter population grows faster than the former. Because such faster population growth accelerates the rise in the fraction's denominator, a smaller reduction in the numerator suffices to halve the proportion.

The other revision backdates the baseline of MDG#1 to 1990, thus envisioning that the halving should take place "between 1990 and 2015" rather than between 2000 and 2015.[5] This revision is significant because, lengthening the period in which population growth occurs, it further inflates the denominator and thereby diminishes even farther the needed reduction in the number of poor and hungry people. The population of the developing countries in 2015 was 144% of what it had been in 1990.[6] Therefore a 28% reduction in the number of poor, to 72% of what it was in 1990, suffices to cut that proportion in half.

While retaining the language of halving the incidence of poverty and hunger, the world's governments had, step by step, diluted their commitment from a 50% reduction during the 1996-2015 period to a 28% reduction during the 1990-2015 period.[7]

While the world's governments were busy diluting their commitments, the number of undernourished people worldwide actually rose. In May 2010, in the context of large increases in food prices that led to food riots in at least 24 countries,[8] the UN Food and Agriculture Organization (FAO) announced that, for the first time in all of human history, more than one billion human beings were undernourished.[9] This announcement was dramatically at odds with the upbeat news propagated by the World Bank, which had been reporting steep declines in extreme poverty. In short order, the FAO was brought into line, compelled to lower its count of the hungry. The FAO did so by revising its definition and methodology. The Economist magazine commented gleefully that the one-billion figure "was completely bogus. This week, in its 2012 report on the state of food insecurity in the world, the FAO quietly revised it down to 868m and got rid of the spike in the numbers that had supposedly occurred in 2008-10."[10] According to the Economist and the disciplined FAO, millions of people marching in the streets because they could not feed their families had been mistaken: there had been no food crisis, no spike in undernourishment.

How did the FAO reduce its count of undernourished people from over one billion to 868 million? It did so by changing its definition of undernourishment. According to its new explication, "undernourishment has been defined as an extreme form of food insecurity, arising when food energy availability [dietary energy intake] is inadequate to cover even minimum needs for a sedentary lifestyle … [for] over a year."[11] By focusing solely on dietary energy intake, this definition ignores problems of food absorption as often associated with parasitic infections. It also defines out of existence all undernourishment due to lacking proteins, vitamins, minerals and other essential micronutrients, even while poverty-related deficiencies in Vitamin A, iron and zinc cause hundreds of thousands of deaths every year. The FAO's definition further ignores that many poor people do hard physical labor to survive. Even if such people ingest sufficient energy to meet the minimum needs for a sedentary lifestyle and are thus counted as adequately nourished by the FAO, they may still die of starvation. All this is topped off by counting as undernourished only those whose energy deficit lasts for at least a year. The FAO defends this by writing: "the reference period should be long enough for the consequences of low food intake to be detrimental to health. Although there is no doubt that temporary food shortage may be stressful, the FAO indicator is based on a full year."[12] Of course the FAO knows better: going hungry for under one year can be very detrimental to health. In fact, it can be fatal. Nonetheless, the FAO's definition ensures that those who die of starvation in less than one year never suffer undernourishment and therefore never show up in its statistics.[13]

Seeing the FAO cave to governmental pressure and seeing it formulate such an utterly absurd definition of undernourishment – this is deeply disturbing. Yet, we should not be surprised. Like all intergovernmental organizations, the FAO is entirely dependent, for its budget and leadership appointments, on national governments, which of course are greatly interested in how the official assessments make them look. If the officers of the FAO want to be effective in protecting undernourished people, agricultural laborers and small farmers, then they must be prepared to lie and cheat for the governments that control their resources. Absurd as its cosmetic efforts are, it is hard to blame the FAO for them.

We can of course blame the governments and politicians of the wealthier countries who are insisting on such cruel deceptions in total indifference to the world's poor. But it is far more important to reflect on our own responsibilities as human beings and citizens of this world. Our responsibility is to be critical of the official stories, especially when it is so obvious that their originators have a vested interest in making themselves and their policies look good without any real expenditure of political capital. Governments assure us that globalization pursuant to the Washington Consensus (as epitomized by the International Monetary Fund, the World Bank and the World Trade Organization) has been good for the world's poor. It is our responsibility to check. This responsibility weighs especially on job-secure academics, who are trained to cut through such deceptions and to develop alternative definitions, methodologies and data. That the dilutions of the international commitments to halve poverty and hunger have remained unnoticed reflects a stunning failure also of economists. Billions of human beings avoidably living and dying in poverty are surely important enough to command serious intellectual attention.

As academics, we must guard and warn against manipulations of four kinds. First, there are outright lies, such as the following graphic from a propaganda video published by Bill Gates and Steven Pinker.[14] In 2015, even by the FAO's absurd definition, 8.3% of the world's population were undernourished and 22.8% were food insecure.[15]

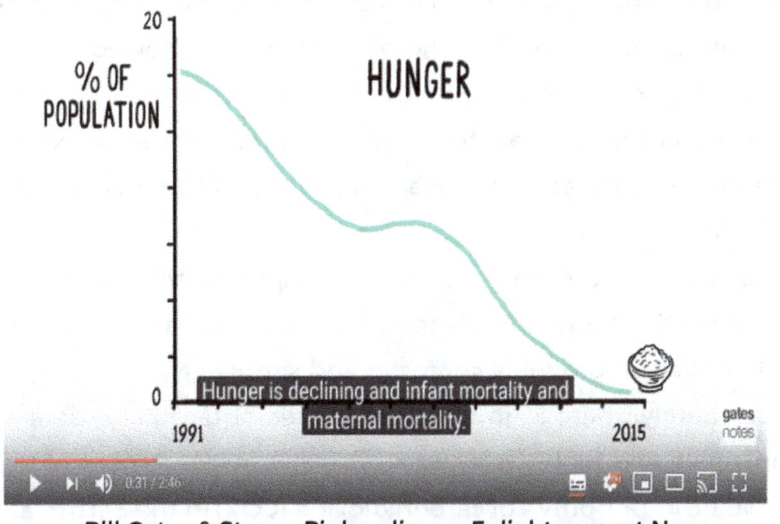

Bill Gates & Steven Pinker discuss Enlightenment Now

Second, there are promises and commitments sold as progress. Governments solemnly announce that something will be achieved decades in the future, thereby luring the public into a false sense of satisfaction and complacency. Pretty much all such official declarations are fraudulent: they are not sincerely intended and will not be fulfilled.

Examples abound. An end of hunger and poverty has been promised many times during the last 80 years. And yet, in 2019, even before COVID struck, the official statistic showed that over 3 billion human beings, 41.9% of those for whom we have data, cannot afford a healthy diet at an average cost of $4 at purchasing power parity[16] – even though the global average income has reached $50 per person per day at purchasing power parity.

That official development assistance would reach 0.7% of the gross national incomes of the affluent countries has been promised again and again since 1970[17] – and yet, despite counting loans and employing various other accounting gimmicks, 50 years later, in the COVID emergency year of 2020, the level is still only 0.32%.[18]

In 2009, at the COP 15 in Copenhagen, the affluent countries solemnly promised that, by 2020, they would be providing at least $100 billion annually to help developing countries mitigate and adapt to climate change, which was overwhelmingly caused by these richer countries. They have had eleven years to build up to fulfilling their promise. And yet, they broke this promise too, even if one includes (as they do) repayable loans in the totals.[19]

Like the Rome Declaration, the Millennium Declaration, the Millennium Development Goals, the Sustainable Development Goals, and the Paris Agreement, such promises and commitments dissipate political pressures and enable politicians to kick the proverbial can down the road. Let future politicians deal with the promise – they can always duck out by explaining that, when the promise was made, they were not yet in office.

The third kind of manipulation is creative accounting of the sorts we have analyzed in connection with the commitment to halve hunger and poverty by 2015. This kind of manipulation is thriving in the aftermath of the Paris Agreement, which allowed every state to formulate its own emissions targets. A government can thus dream up some baseline – some horrendously high level of emissions that its country might have reached at some future time – and can then aim for a "reduction" of that future level, even if it is still an increase over its emissions in the Paris base year of 2015.

The fourth kind of manipulation is simply information overload: inundating the public discourse with such a huge abundance of statistics, data, forecast and conflicting opinions that ordinary citizens are thoroughly confused and simply give up trying to understand what is really going on. Fortunately, there is, in the climate area at least, one data set that is hard to manipulate, highly objective and highly relevant. This is the measurement of the concentration – in parts per million of volume, or ppmv – of carbon dioxide (CO_2) in the Earth's atmosphere. Continuously measured in a sheltered location at Mauna Loa Observatory, Hawaii, this CO2 concentration determines rather precisely how much extra heat energy the Earth picks up from the incoming sunlight. The CO2 concentration was about 280 ppmv in pre-industrial times (before 1750) and has since increased about 50% at an ever-steepening rate.[20] As the nearby graph shows, there is seasonal fluctuation but, thus far, a very steady annual increase. Even with a good magnifying glass, you won't see any effect of the Paris Agreement and of all the many efforts announced with so much fanfare over the years. Keep your eyes on this graph.[21] If you see it curving toward the right, and especially if you see it peak and begin to decline, then you will know that something is actually being done about global warming. Until then, grand rhetoric notwithstanding, our governments and politicians will have accomplished nothing real.

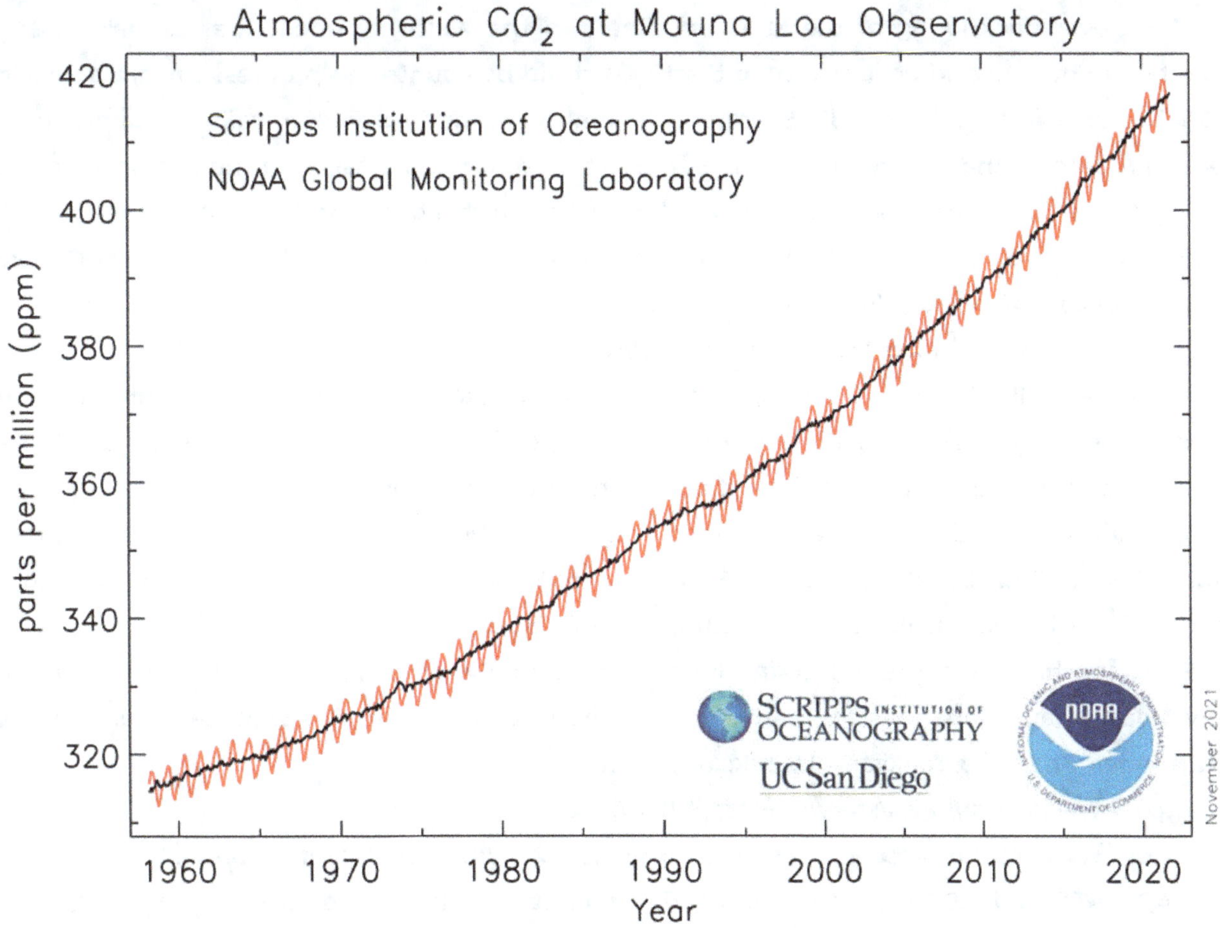

In addition to cutting through the smog of political deception and misinformation, also try to make it harder for politicians to mislead. Politicians are not by nature dishonest, but because we let them get away with it. As an enlightened public, we have the expertise and communications capacities to ensure that more honesty is their best policy. If we each do our share, we can greatly improve our politics and public discourse.

EndNote

[1] https://unfccc.int/process-and-meetings/conferences/past-conferences/paris-climate-change-conference-november-2015/cop-21.

[2] Rome Declaration on World Food Security. November 1996. https://www.fao.org/3/w3613e/w3613e00.htm.

[3] UN Millennium Declaration. September 2000. Article 19. https://www.ohchr.org/EN/ProfessionalInterest/Pages/Millennium.aspx.

[4] See, for example, UN. The Millennium Development Goals Report 2011. http://mdgs.un.org/unsd/mdg/Resources/Static/Products/Progress2011/11-31339%20(E)%20MDG%20Report%202011_Book%20LR.pdf. Pages 6 and 11.

[5] This clever backdating of the MDG baseline had the welcome effect that China's massive reduction in hunger and poverty during the 1990s could be counted as progress toward achieving MDG#1. The revision allowed UN Secretary-General Kofi Annan tragicomically to report to the General Assembly that for the world's most populous region – East Asia and the Pacific – the 2015 poverty target was met already in 1999, a full year before this goal had even been adopted! See Implementation of the United Nations Millennium Declaration: Report of the Secretary-General. https://undocs.org/en/A/57/270. Pages 8 and 22.

[6] https://data.worldbank.org/indicator/SP.POP.TOTL.

[7] Despite all these dilutions, the MDGs ended up mostly unachieved. See https://ourworldindata.org/millennium-development-goals#. The poverty target was counted as achieved, but then the World Bank's definition and measurement of extreme poverty are highly problematic. For a critique, see Sanjay Reddy and Thomas Pogge, "How Not to Count the Poor," in Sudhir Anand, Paul Segal and Joseph Stiglitz, editors: Debates on the Measurement of Global Poverty. Oxford. Oxford University Press 2010. Pages 42–85.

[8] Bangladesh, Bolivia, Brazil, Burkina Faso, Cameroon, Egypt, Ethiopia, Haiti, India, Indonesia, Ivory Coast, Mauritania, Mexico, Morocco, Mozambique, Myanmar, Pakistan, Senegal, Somalia, South Africa, Sri Lanka, Tajikistan, Uzbekistan, Yemen.

[9] http://www.fao.org/news/story/en/item/42158/icode/.

[10] https://www.economist.com/feast-and-famine/2012/10/10/not-a-billion-after-all.

[11] FAO, WFP & IFAD. The State of Food Insecurity in the World 2012. Rome, FAO 2012. https://www.fao.org/3/i3027e/i3027e.pdf. Page 50.

[12] Ibid. Page 50.

[13] The account summarized in this paragraph is based on my much more detailed treatment in Thomas Pogge, "The Hunger Games," Food Ethics 1:1 (2016). Pages 9–27. http://link.springer.com/article/10.1007/s41055-016-0006-9.

[14] This graph is a screengrab from a video Bill Gates and Steven Pinker produced together. https://www.cnet.com/news/bill-gates-favorite-book-enlightenment-now-steven-pinker/. For more on Bill Gates's misrepresentations, see Thomas Pogge, "Fighting global poverty," International Journal of Law in Context 13:4 (2017). Pages 512–526. https://www.cambridge.org/core/journals/international-journal-of-law-in-context/article/fighting-global-poverty/97D5A41BD8EEFF88346C752DB8233053.

[15] FAO, IFAD, UNICEF, WFP and WHO, The State of Food Security and Nutrition in the World 2021, Rome, FAO 2021, https://doi.org/10.4060/cb4474en. Table 1, page 11; and Table 3, page 17.

[16] Ibid. Table 5, page 27.

[17] https://www.oecd.org/development/stats/the07odagnitarget-ahistory.htm#.

[18] https://www.devex.com/news/what-to-make-of-the-2020-dac-stats-99641.

[19] Jocelyn Timperlay, "The broken $100-billion promise of climate finance — and how to fix it." Nature, 20 October 2021. https://www.nature.com/articles/d41586-021-02846-3.

[20] Richard Betts, "Atmospheric CO2 now hitting 50% higher than pre-industrial levels." 16 March 2021. https://www.carbonbrief.org/met-office-atmospheric-co2-now-hitting-50-higher-than-pre-industrial-levels.

[21] https://gml.noaa.gov/ccgg/trends/mlo.html.

HAPPINESS: THE ULTIMATE GOAL OR A BY-PRODUCT

BY SHRISHTI PATEL

So the very basic question I want you to ask yourself first is; what is happiness to you? A certain hobby or a good morning text from a loved one, a satisfactory state of mind or some adventure, your job or a vacation away from your job, a thousand million dollar or a meaningful life. It can be anything as the perspectives and situations differ from person to person.

But let's first talk about what generally nowadays is referred to as happiness which is feeling good all the time. Firstly it's nearly impossible and secondly it's very misleading and wrong. Because if this is right and feeling 'good' is the scale of happiness then we can say that a person consuming cocaine everyday must be the happiest. But what goes up must come down as well. You can never stay in constant happy mode. Recent searches show that if you focus too much on trying to feel good all the time, you'll undermine your capability to feel good at all. In simpler terms, no amount of feeling good will be satisfying to you. If someone experiences happiness all the time day and night, what possibly could motivate him to change their life circumstance or analyse the wrongs about themselves. And also without adversity and struggle humans fails to fully develop themselves intellectually, spiritually and morally. Under this view obstacles must be put in our way by either fate, circumstances or society for us to become the final best versions of ourselves. In this way achievement through adversity or overcoming becomes an integral part of being a successful and fully rounded person and thereby happy in a fuller, Aristotelian world.

Another misconception is being rich and able to afford anything you like or to achieve a certain goal. While such things do make you feel good, there are two possible consequences to it. One is that you might find yourself overindulged in these materialistic pleasures, hence you'll lose growth and after a long time of being stuck in a same place that feeling good emotion will fade away. Other is that you might apart from taking a moment of actually acknowledging the happiness, you strive for more and this hunger for more pleasure never reaches a final destination. So momentary pleasures are not proportional to happiness and If not all this then what is it that can be considered a state of real happiness and how do we achieve it?

Socrates believed that many experiences we might describe as pleasurable, like feeling better after a long illness, were not true happiness – only the absence of suffering.

He thought that happiness should not be based on external things, but on how they are used. For example: Using money to donate to a good cause, using intelligence to solve problems, Using strength for good, and not to manipulate others. So, it's not about what you have – it's about how you use it.

Though the very particular definition of happiness has been a very wide spectrum and even people have been agonising over this definition for centuries. So if you are unable to define happiness properly, you're not alone. All the great philosophers as we've seen Socrates earlier had different take on this and while diving into this we talk about Aristotle.

Philosophers often seem to be in ultimate search of ethics and Aristotle (384- 322 BC) was also not left untouched with this emotion. In one his best-known works in this area, the Nicomachean ethics, written for his son, Nichomachus, he has extensively given emphasis on how should people conduct themselves in every aspect of their life in order to reach their full potential as human beings in order to flourish and thereby achieve true happiness as he said, "one swallow does not make a summer; neither does one day. Similarly neither can one day or a brief space of time make a man blessed and happy." He believed that happiness was the ultimate goal of human existence. Rather than viewing happiness as something you might experience after passing a certain exam or spending time with your loved ones, he described it as a measure of your entire life and how well you've lived it. He looked at it as a goal rather than a momentary feeling.

Similarly Plato (427-347 BC) is also something of an ascetic. He thinks that true happiness can be found in a life of philosophical and spiritual devotion where one avoids the pleasure-pain rollercoaster. He advocates 'living life to the fullest' by building a well-rounded, balanced existence where a person does not deprive himself in one area by overdoing the other.

While Nietzsche believed that happiness was strongly connected to personal agency and the ability to live life the way you wanted to. Nietzsche said, "What is happiness? The feeling that power increases, that resistance is being overcome." He believed that happiness was a kind of power that people could exert over the world around them. This might sound a little sinister, but it could manifest in many innocuous ways. For example, to be happy, you might want the power to: Live in the location you want, Work at a job you enjoy, Have relationships with people of your choice, spend your time in the way you want. When the power to do these things is taken away, we feel unhappy and attempt to take back control.

Kant described it however differently, that the more you make it an ultimate goal or the more you try to be happy, the more unhappy you would find yourself. Have you ever tried so hard to enjoy something that you ended up feeling disappointed or dissatisfied. If yes then you can understand this scenario. Kant said, "Happiness is the satisfaction of all our inclinations". But what exactly are these inclinations? Well, Kant also acknowledges the fact that we don't always know what's best for us, saying that human beings: are not capable of determining with complete certainty ... what will make him truly happy. So by his views, Instead of constantly trying to attain things that we believe will make up happy, Kant says we should focus on acting in the way that we believe is right.

So, in all of the described definitions who would you agree with most? What do you think is the right way to describe happiness? Or would you find a slogan ran by tobacco advertisement in 1966 saying "Happiness is a cigar called Hamlet" more suitable. I think in a state of happiness one would indeed feel oneself to be content, even free. Yet at the same time their ability to examine, criticise and change themselves and the society around them would be sharply curtailed. Happiness should not be a constant emotion neither an ultimate goal. Why? Let's say it's your ultimate goal of life and it's not tough to imagine because everyone wants life to be rainbows and sunshine. So, what if one sceptical day you lose hope of ever achieving it and suddenly you don't want to wake up next morning because you've been living only in the hope of that happiness. You simply cannot lay the foundations of your life in such expectation joy. Because I agree to Kant here as he somewhat described the ultimate happiness to be a mirage that no matter how much you chase after, it'll always seem to be at a distance. And after a long run you'll find yourself tired and dissatisfied and what worse; you might have even missed to feel the few happy moments you countered in life as you were too busy and tempted to reach that ultimate level and same goes for it being a constant emotion as well.

Bringing our discussions to the present day; we are trending toward a hypothetical situation where happiness is all that is targeted. Rather than it should be treated as a by-product. Not necessarily, it has to come along with every action we take because like any other emotion it also comes with a time period. One day you feel happy the next day you might not so let it be a part of your life without clinging on to it. Well maybe happiness lies in the moral functioning and evolution. After all it is the experience of injustice that stimulates the thirst for the opposite; it is the experience of evil that impels us to seek good. Here evils provide us some necessary form of knowledge that leads us to desire the good, a yet higher state of knowledge. In this understanding happiness is a kind of contented wisdom, gathered, in part, from or through prior states of unhappiness. So if you feel sorrowful, dejected or down in the dump, not happy or contented then do not chase after the feeling of happiness but sit relax take some time to reflect and reasons to be grateful. I would say; do not struggle for happiness, except do what you think will make you feel right, morally and individually, let happiness eventually come as a by-product.

MYTHOLOGY

A TRUE NIGHTMARE BEFORE CHRISTMAS

BY WAYNE GARRETH C.

"You better watch out,
You better not cry,
You better not pout,
I'm telling you why..."

Frank Sinatra's legendary Christmas anthem will go down in history for being one of the most popular and well-known tunes played during the yuletide season. While some may see the opening of this song as a cautionary verse to little children everywhere to be on their best behaviour before Christmas, sceptics may analyse this precaution with a grim undertone that others would not this time of year.

Children joyfully look forward to the day Saint Nicholas comes bearing gifts and granting them their most desired presents. Some of them, in fact, wait an entire year for this day. Most can recall beloved characters that accompany Santa on his journey all around the world to bring these little joys to those children that have been, one would call, "nice" during the Christmastime period. Among those characters include Rudolph the Red Nose Reindeer, and a multitude of elves. One creature who joins this annual journey however, may be less embracing than the others who assist jolly ol' Saint Nick for this magical and extraordinary expedition.

Krampus, or as others may know him, The "Anti-Claus", is believed to be the polar opposite of Santa Claus, whom as stated earlier, is Saint Nicholas. The name of this immortal creature comes from the German term Krampen- meaning claw in exact translation. Embracing a dark and horrifying appearance, Krampus is popularly associated with having black fur covering his entire body, cloven hooves as his hands and feet, bulky horns on the top of his head, and having an extensively long red tongue that sprawls out when he gets close to his prey. He is garbed with various chains attached to bells, carrying a whip or a birch used to smite his exploit. Varying accounts also depict Krampus as carrying a large bag or basket for kidnapping young children, while harsher Pagan traditionalists exposit said bag as a medium to drag them to hell instead.

Origins of Krampus varies from one storyteller to the next, often differentiating on the basis of Pagan and Christian traditions. Nevertheless, it seems as though one version carries to the next, with historical provisions adding that while the beginning of the myth of Krampus began pre-Paganism, Catholicism and Christianity had a role in morphing the continual belief and existence of this creature in modern-day society. Pre-Paganism described Krampus as somewhat of a Horned God, associated with nature, sexuality and hunting. Horned Gods also have their roots dug into traditional Wicca. By British Traditional Wicca, these deities are believed to be a dualistic God, carrying both aspects of one personality when carving out their behaviour (ie : night and day, summer and winter). Nonetheless, such a description does little to the aid in the narrative development of Krampus as a conceptualised beast, as his temperament is based primarily on being the opposite of Saint Nicholas, rather than personifying two sides of a singular coin of good and evil.

(Krampus according to his historical depiction, both physically and bearing his accompanied items).

In the era of Paganism, specific celebrations of the winter solstice supported the development and understanding of Krampus being more than just an folklore tied to the Yuletide season. Early representations among certain European countries such as Alpine Austria, Northern Germany and the Czech Republic did not recognise Krampus as the central figure opposing Kris Kringle. Instead, village folklore on the Goddess of Winter, also known as Perchta by the Brothers Grimm, was accepted as a combination of the good and bad during the Christmas period for these locations. This understanding sketches a story similar to that during the pre-Paganism era, where the Horned God was seen as possessing both morality and sin. Some would label her as the embodiment of both Saint Nicholas and Krampus.

According to the Austrian Alpine fable, the Perchta would appear during the Twelve Days of Christmas, overseeing any little boy or girl who slept in their bed awaiting Christmas Day. Summarily, she is believed to leave a silver coin in the shoes of children who were predicated as good that calendar year. However, to those children who had been naughty, she is believed to cut out their stomach and replace it with straw and pebbles while they sleep at night.

The duplexity of Perchta was displayed in her appearance, portrayed as an astonishing beauty in white when visiting good children, and a retched hag with disfigurements and scars when visiting badly behaved children. Resembling Saint Nicholas, Perchta was often accompanied in her journey by the Perchten, a group of spiritual entities who predisposed a duality of exhibition as Perchta herself. The key feature of the Perchten was in their appearance when visiting disobedient children, as they were described as possessing fangs, black fur, tusks and a horse tail, bearing a stark similarity to Krampus himself. Disfigured Perchten however, were believed to ware off bad spirits and protect homes from evil spirits.

Would one feel the taste of irony in the bad spirit somehow being, a naughty child? Maybe so. Even so, this eventually inspired men within communities of Alpine Austria and Germany to dress up as Perchten during the final week of December, visiting houses and occupational buildings to ware off bad energy. This practice came to be known domestically as Perchtenlauf. In modern day adaptation, such a practice has come to be known as the Perchten Run, as the men who partake in these acts often run around their chosen locations in hysterics, often terrifying their fellow inhabitants in the process.

(The Perchta)

Such observances by contrasting European cultures inherently tied the story of Krampus through the eyes of Paganism and Christianity together, though some variations do arise due to what some believe is the church intentionally suppressing the story of Krampus, due to the conservative and orthodox trajectories the institute aimed to project. In spite of that, the attempts of Christian denominations trying to prevent the annual Perchtenlauf was unsuccessful going into the 10th and 11th century. By the 16th century, some form of a compromise was reached between these areas in central Europe and the Orthodox Church.

With the rising popularity in Saint Nicholas as a glorious martyr of the Christmas season by instigation of the church, the institution sought to ban Perchtenlauf permanently, and therefore the belief in Perchten symbolism for Austrian and German villages. Refusing to defeated, these areas, primarily Alpine Austria, generated a variant of the Perchten, which came to be known as Krampus. Commencing this idea in line with their forbidden tradition, Alpine Austria aligned the allegory of Krampus with that of Perchta while simultaneously connecting their Pagan beliefs with that of the Orthodox Church, initially to stimulate irritation among the religious community.

The Feast of Saint Nicholas is celebrated on December 6th yearly, offering up Kris Kringle in the same fashion the church would for any other saint in practice. Through such a devout day of reverence came the eve of mischief and disobedience. The preceding evening of the Feast of Saint Nicholas, December 5th, has come to be known as Krampus Night, or as called customarily, Krampusnacht. Such an evening details for the night which the wicked creature appears on the streets, terrifying children and adults alike.

Horrifying, is it not? Maybe in practice, but not in actual display. As somewhat of a constituent of Krampusnacht, a disorganised "run" was used as a tool by rowdy and reckless men to dress up as the horrifying creature to terrorise the town of which they inhabited, which is known as Krampuslauf. Individuals often dawned a disfigured goat mask, a large fur coat, and a whip or tree branch; creating a costume similar to the actual appearance of the Christmas Demon. Dressed and ready, these individuals would often then go on a "run", terrorising their Austrian village, namely homes and certain businesses. The term run was represented colloquially, as those who partook in Krampuslauf literally ran around their village, some of those time committing property damage wherever they chose.

(Public participation in a modern day Krampuslauf, dressed in the believed depiction of Krampus himself).

While true to form and what some may go further to consider as venerating Krampus and keeping the tradition of the Perchten alive, this custom was done to defy and disobey the reverence of the church towards Saint Nicholas. Despite that, somewhat of a buffer was exhumed by the Austrians to prevent this tradition from being outright banned as Perchten was, by having individuals dress up as Saint Nicholas to accompany Krampus, therefore providing some essence of neutrality between the Christmas Demon and Father Christmas. Though not ideal, the church sought this as an opportunity to direct an account of this newly found tradition, merging Krampus and Saint Nicholas to a Yin Yang position ; representing both reward and punishment. Krampus was now morphed into becoming a version of the Christmas Devil, with his chains, as stated earlier, binding him to the church. The characterisation of Krampus has undergone a shift in modern time, often with the tale being directed to a more sinister and appalling undertone. From beating children with a whip or giving them coal for Christmas, the tale of Krampus goes as far as to drown naughty children or smother them in their sleep.

This practice of Krampuslauf has continued to present day. The expansion of this practice has come to include carrying out this tradition on Christmas Eve for those celebrating Christmas outside the Alpine Austrian region. While some choose to harmlessly scare a person that comes their way, others whip children at the back of their leg, even going as far as to visit certain houses to terrorise children and adults alike. In Styria, located in southeast Austria, mothers often paint twigs gold and display them around the house year round as a reminder to young children to be good in order to prevent a visit from Krampus. The celebration of Krampusnacht and the practice of Krampuslauf has extended to regions of North America, Australia and even East Asia, providing a fun yet spine-tingling event for those overcome with a different kind of Christmas Spirit.

(Example of a Krampuskarten, often given during the Christmas season)

Pop culture and the holiday season has also grown to adapt Krampus in the celebration present day. Greeting cards with Krampus persecuting and tormenting children, that have come to be known as Krampuskarten, were made popular in the 1800s. This has continued to present day with many individuals choosing this option as a holiday greeting rather than virtuous, upstanding cards with Father Christmas. The devilish creature was also highlighted in the Christmas comedy film after his name in 2015, starring Academy Award nominated actress Toni Collette.

Ultimately, Krampus may be more of a misunderstood being by audiences everywhere. Though there lies a misty undertone to himself as a caricature and those who claim to have inspired his creation, a symbol of pure evil or as more commonly known, The Christmas Devil, is a harsh overstatement of his demeanour. Acting as a companion to Saint Nicholas after the Christianisation of Alpine Austria, his tradition goes hand-in-hand with the work of Santa himself, while only punishing those guilty by behaviour during the Christmas season. A requisite evil, one might say? With that, I leave you, the reader to decide during this Crimbo.

WHY DID MATA SATI DESTROY HER BODY?

BY TRUPTI REKHA DASMAHAPATRA

When the universe was created, Prajapati Daksh was assigned with the role of a caretaker of all human beings that were created by Lord Brahma and he was also a wiser and one of the favorite sons of Lord Brahma. He was one of the greatest devotees of Lord Vishnu. As the Prajapati, he implemented certain rules for the society which were obeyed by everyone except Lord Shiva. He was not aligned with the concept adopted by Lord Shiva. He believed Lord Shiva was his enemy and he never respected him.

The fact is that when the universe is created, Prakriti (Nature) and Purush (Male) are being created. Purush divided himself into three parts and they are Lord Brahma, Lord Vishnu and Lord Shiva. Prakriti or Shakti divided herself into three parts and they are Mata Saraswati, Mata Lakshmi and Mata Parvati (Form of Mata Sati or Adi Shakti). Every Shakti is assigned with different powers. Mata Saraswati is the owner of Knowledge (Gyan), Mata Lakshmi is the owner of Wealth (Dhan) and Mata Parvati is the owner of Shakti (Power). When Adi Shakti takes human form, she took birth as the daughter of Prajapati Daksh.

When Lord Brahma created this creation, he requested Lord Shiva to give Shakti (Adi Shakti) for the betterment of the universe. Lord Shiva sacrificed Shakti (Adi Shakti) from himself for the betterment of the universe. At that time, Daksh (yet to become Prajapati) pleased Adi Shakti with his hard penance and requested her to be born as his daughter and he would give her hands to Lord Shiva. Adi Shakti blessed him with his wish. Everyone knows Mata Sati was the daughter of Prajapati Daksh but originally she was Adi Shakti...wife of Lord Shiva.

When she attained her maturity, she was extraordinarily fascinated by Lord Shiva without knowing the origin of her birth. She found a Rudrakshya from a river and wished to keep it with her. But her sisters told that Lord Shiva was their enemy and Rudrakshya is the symbol of Lord Shiva. As the devotee of Lord Vishnu, they should not encourage any object that belongs to Lord Shiva.

As time passed, Mata Sati felt extraordinary attraction towards Lord Shiva and was extremely confused about her feelings towards him. She thought she was proceeding against her father and considered herself as an inefficient daughter. She was frequently getting the dream of a dancing human who has a half female and half male body. This dream increased her anxiety to an extreme level. She tried to find out the fact but couldn't find an answer. On the other side, Lord Shiva knew all the truth and he knew Mata Sati (Adi Shakti) is his wife but he denied marrying her when Lord Vishnu and Lord Brahma requested him to get married to Mata Sati. The question is when Lord Shiva knows Mata Sati is Adi Shakti, his wife then what can be the reason for not accepting her? Prajapati Daksh established Lord Vishnu's temple where a huge statue of Lord Vishnu has to be fixed, but a lot of crowds couldn't move the statue into the temple. Prajapati Daksh conducted a Maha Yagnya with the presence of all the greatest pandits to please Lord Vishnu. Still, no one could move the statue. The great sages knew the reason for this unsuccessful effort. The real reason for not moving the statue is the absence of ShivLing. The concept of Tridev is completed with the presence of Lord Brahma, Lord Vishnu and Lord Shiva. Prajapati Daksh kept the statue of Lord Brahma with Lord Vishnu but ShivLing was not there. In order to complete the process of Yagnya Mata Sati went to the river Saraswati to bring water but she ended up reaching the place where there is the Ashram of Dadhichi. Sage Dadhichi explained to Mata Sati the reason for the stagnant statue of Lord Vishnu. That is why Mata Sati kept a small Shiv Ling near the statue of Lord Vishnu with a lot of courage. Then the statue of Lord Vishnu became movable when the crowd tried moving the statue. But Prajapati Daksh got angry when he saw the ShivLing near the statue of Lord Vishnu and wished to know the person who kept it. Mata Sati dared to say that she had kept the ShivLing near to the statue. Consequently, she was punished by her father. The punishment was to collect 1lakh Lotus and to write Lord Vishnu's name on every petal. Mata Sati promised herself to accept this punishment and completed all tasks given by Prajapati Daksh. Once all tasks were completed, Prajapati Daksh wanted to see Lord Vishnu's name on the petals but he got angry when he saw the name of Lord Shiva written on every lotus petals. Mata Sati asked Prajapati Daksh to forgive her for this mistake. But she couldn't understand how the name of Lord Vishnu was changed into Lord Shiva. Though Mata Sati was fascinated by the name of Lord Shiva again and again, she couldn't accept this bitter truth. As a Dakshyaini she should be the devotee of Lord Vishnu.

On the other hand, Tadakashur was trying to kill Mata Sati. He was blessed from Lord Shiva that no one could kill him apart from Lord Shiva's son and he knew that Mata Sati is Adi Shakti who is going to be the wife of Lord Shiva. When he attacked Mata Sati, every time Lord Shiva saved her. This activity of Lord Shiva proved his love towards Mata Sati. When all devas requested Lord Shiva to marry Mata Sati, he denied it. Lord Brahma and Lord Vishnu also visited Kailash to approach the same. Still, Lord Shiva denied. The real reason behind it is his love for Adi Shakti Mata Sati. When Lord Vishnu asked him the reason for his refusal, Lord Shiva explained that he is Jagat Pita (Father of the Universe) and he has all responsibility to manage the creation (this world) where he has to bear a lot of pain. He doesn't want Adi Shakti to go through the same pain as his wife. Also, Lord Shiva knew that Mata Sati will not survive if she gets married with him.

Prajapati Daksh came to know about the love Mata Sati has in her heart towards Lord Shiva. So he tried to give Mata Sati's hand to a handsome and courageous prince as soon as possible. He wanted to conduct a Swayamber for Mata Sati and gave the rights to choose her husband as per her wish. Various princes were invited to participate in it. But on the day before the Swayamber, Prajapati Daksh asked a sculptor to make a statue of Lord Shiva and placed it at the door of

Swayamber hall as a gatekeeper. He thought it will be a great insult to Lord Shiva. When Mata Sati came to Swayamber hall with the garland, she saw the statue and put the garland on the neck of Lord Shiva's statue and prayed wholeheartedly to appear. Lord Shiva appeared and accepted this relationship but Prajapati Daksh did not accept this marriage as Mata Sati put garland on the neck of a statue. When Lord Vishnu asked Prajapati Daksh to accept this marriage, he couldn't avoid it. At last, Prajapati Daksh accepted this relationship but not heartily.

Lord Shiva and Mata Sati departed to Kailash from Prajapati Daksh's palace. But Prajapati Daksh did not leave his ego and wanted to take revenge on Lord Shiva. In order to insult Lord Shiva and Mata Sati, he conducted a Maha Yagyan where all Devas and Devis were invited except Lord Shiva and Mata Sati. Mata Sati wanted to come to Maha Yagyan but Lord Shiva (Mahadev) denied her with a view to go there uninvited. But she wanted to go there somehow and did not hear Lord Shiva's words. As a protector, Lord Shiva sent Nandi (Lord Shiva's greatest devotee) with Mata Sati to Prajapati Daksh's palace. As soon as Mata Sati reached there, Prajapati Daksh started scolding Lord Shiva pointing at his attire, living style and his ornaments. He didn't offer any havan (a fire ritual performed on special occasions by a Hindu priest) to him. When Mata Sati wanted to explain, Prajapati Daksh started insulting Lord Shiva and Mata Sati in front of everyone. Consequently, Mata Sati got angry and turned into her Adi Shakti form. She told to Prajapati Daksh that if she wanted she could kill him within a fraction of a second but she will not do the same as Prajapati Daksh is the father of her physical form. Because of her body, she was listening insulting words casted at her husband. That is why she would burn her body. Consequently, Mata Sati burnt her body throwing herself to the fire that was in Yagyan Kunda (Yagyan pot).

We all know this reason for Mata Sati's death but the real reason is Mata Sati was a human and she was not eligible for Lord Shiva. She should have gone through a lot of purification processes to become eligible. Lord Shiva is a powerful energy which is extraordinary. To become eligible, Mata Sati should have done a lot of sadhanas (efforts) to bear the unseen powerful energy of Lord Shiva. This was the reason Lord Shiva was not ready to marry Mata Sati. But Lord Vishnu requested Lord Shiva to train her and make her eligible. Lord Shiva tried to train her but had an unsuccessful attempt. Mata Sati was Adi Shakti but her human nature suppressed her heavenly or godly nature. She got Lord Shiva as her husband but couldn't resist the power of him. That is the reason, in the next birth, Adi Shakti took birth as a daughter of Him Naresh and her name was Parvati. She had to do Penance for several years to achieve Lord Shiva through which she purified herself and made herself eligible for Lord Shiva. With all the rituals and culture Lord Shiva got married to Mata Parvati. All devas including Lord Vishnu and Lord Brahma were also happy as she completed all levels of penance and there was no fear of destruction of Mata Parvati.

LITERATURE

MORE THAN ESCAPISM: FANTASY SPACES IN CHILDREN'S LITERATURE

BY AASHNA NAGPAL

Fantasy and children's literature have become so inextricably linked that one is often confused with the other. It has been noted that many of the children's books are also fantasy novels and much of fantasy is written taking children as their target audience. Children's literature is a recent phenomenon, flourishing greatly in the late nineteenth and early twentieth century and its deep relation with fantasy is even more new.

Fantasy is about strange worlds with even stranger characters. This genre is mostly associated with magic, adventure, speaking animals and other supernatural elements. A fantasy tale tells a story, or depicts events and adventures, involving magic, alternate worlds, or both, so that the story could not take place in the "real world."[1]. There is a deliberate attempt to violate what's "normal" and logic isn't only challenged but defied. In most cases, fantasy spaces are very different from ordinary spaces which show a conscious attempt of the author to defamiliarise the readers. Fantasy is described as "imaginative fiction dependent for effect on strangeness of setting (such as other worlds or times) and characters (such as supernatural beings)"[2]. Fantasy is a sort of carnival, where anything can happen and the rules of the real world don't uphold. But fantasy tries to build an alternate reality which comes with its own rules, however strange they may be. It builds an entire universe of its own, which sometimes feeds on the distortion of sense of our universe. Children's literature, which swings between didactic and entertaining, uses fantasy as a natural choice because it offers precisely what children yearn- the spirit of endless possibilities and incessant need to play. It's often thought children embrace fantasy because they fail to distinguish between real and unreal. On the contrary, their inclination to fantasy owe to their openness in exploring the fantasy spaces and appreciating the "anything can happen" environment instead of ridiculing it.

Works of literature like Through the Looking Glass and The Wizard of Oz suggest elements of fantasy in their title itself. Going "through" a glass or talking about a wizard hints the readers to expect magic in the story. Mostly, when fantasy and children's literature intertwine, the central character is often a child who gains the reader's sympathy in some way. Dorothy misses her home and longs to be in Kansas again with her uncle and aunt and cries several times throughout the book. Alice, even though a mischievous character, earns the sympathy when the reader realizes she has no one to play with. Similarly, Harry Potter is an orphan who is mistreated by his relatives and the Pevensie children from The Chronicles of Narnia have to stay away from their parents because of an ongoing war with no certainty of ever reuniting with them. This sympathy often helps the young readers to associate themselves with the central character and identity with them. The lonely principal character(s) transcend into a fantasy space, often not deliberately. This change of space is essential for elements of fantasy to function and happens through some sort of a portal like the looking glass in Through the Looking glass, the cyclone in The Wizard of Oz, the wardrobe in The Chronicles of Narnia, Platform 9 3/4 in Harry Potter or the rabbit hole in Alice's Adventures in the Wonderland.

These otherwise ordinary characters, upon transcending to the alternate reality find themselves to be of utmost importance in that universe. They go on to possessing power which the 'real' world doesn't allow them. The power they gain is often earned by defeating or challenging a pre-existing evil authority in that universe. Harry Potter is a celebrity before he even enters the magical world and the Pevensie children are prophesied to become Kings and Queens. Alice's entire journey in the Looking glass world revolves around her wanting to be a Queen. When she's crowned as one towards the end of the book, she sits between the adult Red and White Queen, she feels at par with the adults. She doesn't like that only the Red Queen gives orders and so she gives them too. An important question that troubles Alice is "who it was that dreamed it all?" She wouldn't like to be a part of the Red King's dream because it implies that she lacks power and would not like to be a subject in another's world. Dorothy, even though never officially crowned, becomes a figure of power when she's in possession of both the golden cap and the silver shoes.

When the central character wins a war or asserts their identity in an impactful way in the fantasy space, the young reader who identifies with this character feels the pleasure of possession of such kind of power as well. It provides them with the feeling of triumph and feeds on their desire for power and agency.

Alice's favorite phrase is 'Let's pretend' where she wants to spend her time playing make-believe games. Visit any preschool classroom during free play and you will likely see a child pretending to be someone else. Make-believe play is a ubiquitous part of early childhood[3]. The young reader "construct(s) a new reality, one that conforms to his (or her) own needs and desires"[4] through these make-believe games.

These alternate realities created by fantasy novels take these make-believe games of children to another level by making them more 'real'. This happens because the central character actually enters a fantasy space instead of just pretending. Alice who wanted to 'pretend' to be Kings and Queens with her sister actually goes on a quest to become a Queen. Alice who pretends to be in conversation with her kitten goes into a fantasy space where animals actually reply back. Children who would bring all kinds of props, costumes to make their make-believe games more real would feel captivated on seeing such fantasy spaces actualize in the novels. Dorothy encounters a scarecrow, a tin man, a lion who not only just speak but display human emotions.

Children are often restricted to their homes because it's unsafe for them to go out on their own. Much of children's literature which makes use of fantasy involves a journey in a unique setting. This works on the desire of the young reader to go out and explore, preferably without the supervision of an adult who tells them what and how to do all the time. Alice is glad that "there'll be no one here to scold" her in the Looking glass world. Fantasy offers children a rehearsed exploration of the too big, too wide, too dangerous world that is getting closer and more real every day[5].

Fantasy spaces completely distort the conventional sense of time, space and distance. Alice walking backwards to approach the Red Queen, staying put in the same place despite running fast; Hermione's time turner, the Pevensie children returning to their exact ages on coming out of the land of Narnia to when they had gone in or Dorothy landing in a place so excluded from the rest of the world where they still have wizards and witches- all of these resonate of worlds gone topsy-turvy. Alice makes her journey through a large game of chess in the looking glass world but there are violations of the game- there's a system yet there's none. This tells how fantasy spaces allow children to not abandon logic, but make their own kind of logic. It allows the young readers enough space to come out of the logic that the real world imposes on them. Red Queen becomes a kitten, White Queen becomes a sheep in Through the Looking glass or Dorothy being transported to wherever she wants by knocking the heels together thrice or Harry being a wizard himself perpetuates the idea of magic in fantasy spaces. This isn't just to enchant the children who read them but the idea here is again power to do 'anything' and magic in the hands of the central character makes that happen. When a child who is unable to get hold of a cookie jar at the top shelf reads a book where magic makes everything happen for the central character, it isn't surprising why magic is deliberately infused into the text by writers of children's literature. There is also a deliberate destabilization of language which becomes a medium through which the author and the characters question the laws that govern the adult world.

The adults often make a conscious effort to exclude children from details of war and violence to protect their 'innocence' as justification. With fantasy spaces, the young central character enters war torn spaces and are witness to violence. Through the character of Alice, Carroll dismantles the idea of a child being innocent. Dorothy witnesses beheading of several animals by the tin man and even kills the wicked witch by melting her. Lucy, Adam, Peter and Susan from The Chronicles of Narnia participate in a war themselves and are witness to bloodshed. Adults normally don't imagine children being in situations where it is a matter of life and death. Through these alternative realities, children enter such forbidden situations.

Although Lewis Carroll's Through the Looking glass can be called non-didactic endless play, fantasy is also often used in children's literature to bring about issues of real consequence through metaphors and allegories. This allows the author to bring such issues in a more playful manner for the young readers.

Fantasy is often labeled as a mere attempt to escape reality and this perception is a reason why fantasy is often looked down upon. Despite the fact that fantasy normally functions in another world of its own, fantasy uses this defamiliarizing quality to comment on what's familiar. One needs to understand that something is fantasy only because there's an idea of real and instead of escaping reality, fantasy highlights different aspects of reality itself. An alternate reality is created and through allegory, it enables us to understand the real world better. Fantasy doesn't abandon the real but distorts it, only to make it clearer. The purpose of fantasy is not to escape reality but to illuminate it: to transport us to a world different from the real world, yet to demonstrate certain immutable truths that persist even there- and in every possible world[6]. It's not possible, even for young readers, to read a fantastical text in isolation of their understanding of reality. Fantasy is a violation of certain natural rules which implies there is a perception regarding natural laws or reality in the first place.

Fantasy often leads to insights about the real world. It is through fantasy that we have always sought to make sense of the world, not through reason[7]. While it may offer temporary escape to the reader, immersion into another character and in another world often leads to better self-awareness by making the reader more empathetic. This immersion in fantasy spaces need not imply evasion of everyday life but a complex attempt to comprehend the real world. Many works of fantasy comment on detailed observations of human behavior through strange characters. Fantasy is not a transient tool for the destruction of self or reality of the reader because it helps to accept, tackle and confront it. Fairytales perhaps explain this dichotomy best; despite being the quintessential form of escapist writing, they are layered with universal and timeless life lessons[8]. Fantasy with its infinite scope of possibilities lay open the not so visible layers of contemporary reality by expanding the vision through which the reader looks at the world. Thus, interpreting fantasy as mere escape is fallacious.

Fantasy is an intrinsic part of children's literature not just because many of their generic elements overlap each other but because they complement each other. This combination will continue to evolve with the growing demand of fantasy spaces in works meant for young readers.

EndNote

[1] Defining Fantasy by Steven S. Long

[2] Merriam- Webster's Encyclopedia of Literature

[3] Why make believe play is an important part of childhood, by Tracy Gleason in The Conversation

[4] Imagination and Creativity in Childhood by LEV SEMENOVICH VYGOTSKY

[5] The real purpose of fantasy, by Beth Webb in The guardian

[6] Sheila Egoff, 134, quoted by Zipes

[7] Why Fantasy Matters So Much by Jack Zipes

[8] Literary or Not- The Reality of Escapist Fiction by Sana Hussain in The Missing Slate

ART HISTORY

PUTTING THE ANIMATION INTO ARCHIVES

BY STEPHANIE MARRIE

When the average person hears the word "animation," they think of silly cartoons babysitting their children in place of a working teenager. Said average person, more often than not, is a disapproving parent who cannot believe that their grown children are still watching cartoons rather than the more socially acceptable live-action shows. However, even cursory research will reveal that animation not only has a rich, international, and multifaceted history but also has been put to great use through a variety of methods. Anything with a rich history is worthy of being preserved in an archival repository.

Animation has held an ambivalent place within cinema, considered a novelty at best and a distraction at worst. Rebekah Taylor, the Archives and Special Collections Manager at the University for the Creative Arts, claims that animation is marginalized as a discipline because it is "seen by many as irrelevant and a discipline that is entirely separate from more 'conventional' forms of visual art practice" (8). Yet Taylor says in response to that view, "animation has never been MORE relevant – look at 3D digital animation and modeling...moreover, 2D acetate cels are still used within animation and design. Besides, it is still important to document the history of other techniques within the visual arts that are only rarely used" (8). Truer words were never articulated, as can be seen by the study and subsequent use of old-fashioned 2D animation techniques in the 2017 videogame Cuphead. Taylor adds, "there's a general lack of awareness –many people I've spoken to during my research don't even realize that dedicated animation archives exist" (8). Archivists are not the only ones with concerns about animation in archival memory.

Animation scholars have long attempted to keep the memory of it alive. One such scholar, Paul Wells, notes that animation even today is considered "a lost thing, a perennial outsider" (5). He describes how animation is often marginalized at film awards, "when an animated film of any sort, and about any subject, is finally celebrated it is recognized for its narrative or content, and rarely for its status as 'animation'" (Wells 6). He then puts forth some reasons as to why animation has largely gone unrecognized as a form, despite being the most inclusive of all the art disciplines. One reason is that it has been misunderstood to be "mainly as a children's entertainment" (Wells 7). It does not help matters that some of the most widely circulated seminal animated works are the Disney films, based on simple fairytales meant to be read to children before bedtime and containing the kind of shallow sentimentality one would find reading a Hallmark card. Yet there is much more to animation than Americanized fare such as the Disney films. Wells argues that animation, rather than being an exclusively childish genre, is in reality "a radical and progressive art form and practical application" (7). Animation makes up an international, political archive that should be treated with the same respect as archiving as literary manuscripts.

Today animation is everywhere. It can be found on television, advertisements, mobile phones, documentaries, social networks, movies, video games, and on the web. However, animation need not be limited to mindless entertainment. Reproductive health scholar Shweta Krishnan says, "Animation has been seen as a potential tool for advocacy since UNICEF used it in the late 1960s" (128). Stefanie Van de Peer adds:

The art of animation is often employed as a means to an end: entrepreneurs, politicians, ad military organizations regularly use it to their advantage, whether it is to earn money or propagate a certain ideal. In addition, as the form continues to prove popular, it is being used increasingly as a medium through which to inform, as it was during the early years of cinema (159).

This alone makes up an excess of information that could potentially archived. Being potentially politically charged, animated archives provide uniquely accessible insights into other countries. Yet there are many areas where visual arts research has generally been lacking.

There has been little research on the development of animation outside of cinema and little awareness of how animation developed in countries other than America. For example, according to researcher of early British animation Malcolm Cook, "the lightning cartoon act has received little attention in scholarly work on music hall, despite the act being a popular part of the music hall bill in Britain in the 1880s and 1890s" (237). This lack of awareness is not helped by the fact that "very few direct traces of lightning cartoon acts exist" (Cook 237). Luckily, what little there is left has been preserved by new resources, such as the digitized database of local newspapers held by the British Library, "which allow the use of full text search to pinpoint scarce references, discovery of a significant private collection of material held by the daughter of one of the lightning cartoonists discussed in the article" (Cook 237-8). The importance of up-to-date facilities cannot be underestimated in a scenario such as this.

The lightning cartoon is easily identifiable. At its most basic, the lightning cartoon act is "a performance of the cartoonist providing a drawing…The artist would stand in front of a chalkboard, sheet of paper, or even a canvas, and rapidly produce a drawing…most commonly of public figures in the political or entertainment realm" (Cook 241). In one instance, Little Erskine, a popular cartoonist, "made particular effort to get photographs of local figures, such as the Mayor of Portsmouth, in advance of a visit, to allow him to draw a figure of local significance as port of his act" (Cook 239). The unifying feature of the lightning cartoon was the "lightning speed with which the images were made" (Cook 241). Political figures routinely depicted included "Disraeli" and "Gladstone," though it is not clear just how much political commentary there was on these men

(Cook 239). Based on the remaining descriptions from reviewers at the time: "while addressing vaguely topical issues, acts avoided overt commentary or partisanship…they do not show any indication that the drawings were anything more than gently physical caricatures" (Cook 240). This would suggest that British people around the turn of the century generally liked and did not wish to offend their political figures. Yet if readers take the context of the audience in the music hall, there is more political commentary than at first glance. According to scholar Peter Bailey, who describes an audience commentary on cartoonist Tom Merry's act:

The partisans of Mr. Gladstone cheered when Mr. Tom Merry sketched his portrait, and his opponents of the Jingo tribe howled. They changed their howlings to applause when the late Earl Beaconsfield's visage was drawn; some applauded Bradlaugh's countenance, and some raved over Salisbury and that rash young man Lord Randolph Churchill (Cook 240).

The last key element of the lightning cartoon was "transformation." Transformation was a technique that anticipated the animated cartoons of the early twentieth century, such as father of American animation James Stuart Blackton's Humorous Phases of Funny Faces and the Fleischer Brothers' "Out of the Inkwell" series. According to Cook:

Transformation is often seen as one of the defining characteristics of animation, the malleability and control afforded to the animator courtesy of its frame-by-frame construction allowing unlimited manipulation of the visual field. While the lightning cartoon act does not afford the performer the same degree of control over the visual image as animated cartoons, there is nevertheless some evidence that performers did strive towards the same qualities that would be realized in animated cartoons (247).

A number of acts used transformation as part of their routine, notably Miss Lydia Dreams' act, in which "a portrait of Bismarck is quickly changed into a likeness of Lord Salisbury" (Cook 247). Early animation in Russia was about as tame as early animation in Britain.

In Russia, early animation was very much considered a frivolous novelty. As far as the Soviet discourse goes,

there was a considerable tendency towards regarding animation as either a cinema's servant performing the facilitating functions — creating intertitles or illustrative images of objects and phenomena that could not be reproduced by photographic means — or as a means of entertainment and indirect propaganda capable of producing short satirical films (Blackledge 112).

In 1933, some animation studios put out works that used a variety of techniques, including paper drawings, cut-outs, and flat marionettes. However, by 1936, these small Moscow animation studios were merged with a newly founded major animation studio, Soiuzmul'tfil'm, which worked exclusively with the celluloid (or cel for short) technique. The cel technique is comprised of the layering of the animated image, and it was used to create industrial animation, i.e. animation produced by a conveyor-belt-style assembling of the animated image. Both Walt Disney studios and Fleischer Studios employed this method of production back in America.

Soiuzmul'tfil'm was not the first Soviet animation studio that used the cel technique for animation production. According to scholar Olga Blackledge:

It had been implemented two years earlier at the Experimental Animation Studio at the Scientific-Research Department of GUKF...the head of which, Viktor Smirnov...studied the cel technique of animation production in the USA at the Disney and Fleischer studios in 1933. Thus, in 1933, Soviet animation began moving away from the diversity of animation techniques and styles to a unified production style that employed celluloid, attempting, in part, to cultivate a more unified animation aesthetics (Blackledge 112).

This unification may have made for a more efficient business model, but it came at the cost of artistic diversity that stifled the medium as it took form in Russia, which caused it to, for a while, remain in America's shadow.

Soviet film director Lev Kuleshov provided an alternative viewpoint that was unpopular with Russian officials in his time. In the fall of 1938, the famous Soviet film director Lev Kuleshov gave four lectures to a group of animators working at the central Soviet animation studio Soiuzmul'tfil'm. At this point, the studio already had several animated shorts under their belt. Kuleshov had been invited to give feedback on the studio's films and to teach the animators how to improve their work. After watching the short films, Why Rhino's Skin Has Folds? (Pochemu u nosoroga shkura v skladkakh?) and The Three Musketeers (Tri mushketera), he praised them for being competently made but noted the absence of color. In his eyes, black-and-white films were obsolete after Disney. He also lamented that the films "do not engage with what is topical and important for the Soviet people: improvement of Soviet life, the threat of war, and other such themes" (Blackledge 110). Finally, Kuleshov pointed out that the films were derivative, repeating other films by "employing 'old overused rhymes and unoriginal overused images' in their desire to compete with Disney" (Blackledge 110). For Kuleshov, this direction towards competition with Disney was a "dead end, the only escape from which would be to find an original idea that would drive the creative work" (Blackledge 111). Animation scholars and animators alike agreed with Kuleshov that Russian animation need not be limited to copying other countries' style or fulfilling a narrow function but was versatile and could be used for a variety of topics. Although Russia's early output seemed relatively tame and derivative, animation works from other countries seem to have had heavier, more overt political commentary and attempted to branch out of the Disney style while also taking inspiration from it.

Take China for example, which has long been in Japan's shadow (like the rest of Asia) when it comes to internationally renowned animation. The founding fathers of Chinese animation were the Wan Brothers, who made the first feature length animated film in Asia titled Princess Iron Fan in 1941. Audiences at the time simultaneously lauded the film as progressive anti-Japanese propaganda and regarded the film as a downgrade from 1937's Snow White, which was in full color. According to scholar Daisy Yan Du,

The Wan Brothers' encounter with Hong Kong has been neglected in studies of both Chinese animation and postwar Hong Kong cinema. On the one hand, studies of Chinese animation always focus on the National Style and Chineseness, deliberately disavowing the transnational movements that have contributed to the rise of national cinema and national culture. On the other hand, studies of postwar Hong Kong cinema usually focus on live-action feature film and neglect animation, which is overshadowed by the internationally renowned kung fu and martial arts films (141).

In the history of Asian animation, there has been a noticeable back and forth between China and Japan during the second world war; Japan responded to the advent of Chinese propaganda animation by making their own Disney-esque milestones. "The travel of Princess Iron Fan to Tokyo in 1942," Du continues, "triggered the birth of Momotaro's Sea Eagles (1943) and Momotaro's Divine Sea Warriors (the first animated feature film in Japan) and later inspired Tezuka Osamu to create his Astro Boy (1963)" (141). Later on, the Wan Brothers had planned to complete a film in the postwar era with war still fresh in their memory.

The World of Insects, their unfinished animated film, was going to be an allegory for Japan's invasion of China. It was to be based on the old Aesop fable The Grasshopper and the Ant. It was never finished because "the production of a cel animated feature film at that time was very expensive," and keep in mind, even makers of live-action films were regularly scrimping to save money after the country had been ravaged by the Sino-Japanese war (Du 144). The planned plot of the film is as follows:

The film is about two groups of insects: good and diligent bees pitted against lazy grasshoppers who try to exploit and take advantage of the bees. A human boy named Xiaoniu/Little Ox sides with the bees and helps them in their final battle against the grasshoppers and their allies...the grasshoppers allude to the Japanese while the bees symbolize the hard-working Chinese during the war (Du 144).

This idea was created decades before Disney Pixar's A Bug's Life, which featured a similar plot, but with ants instead of bees. This was a war propaganda film that could have become an important milestone in the history of Chinese animation (like Snow White was to American animation).

Japan has occupied a much more prominent place in animation history than China due to the recent popularity of anime in America. American children of the 1990s grew up watching the show Pocket Monsters (or Pokémon for short), which originated from Japan and became famous enough to be referenced by the more adult-oriented cultural juggernaut The Simpsons. The following incident is where the stereotype of Japanese seizure-inducing anime from the Simpsons episode "The Simpsons Go to Japan" comes from: the distribution and subsequent banning of the episode "Electric Solider Porygon." The episode's infamous climax plays out as follows:

The action takes place inside the hard drive of a computer, where teenage warriors aided by the Pokemon they train have descended to battle computer viruses. The enemy viruses fire missiles and the Pokemon Pikachu responds by emitting bolts of electricity that produce thunderous explosions upon impact with the oncoming missiles. The blast fills the entire screen. A burst of white is followed by rapid flashes of blue, red, and violet colors. Then a bigger explosion covers the frame with clouds of black smoke. In the final scene, the teenage warriors emerge dumbfounded (along with the victorious Pokemon) from the burned ruins of the building where the computer was located (Papapetros 301).

The aforementioned rapid flashes caused mass seizures among both Japanese and American children, to the point where years later, one of the show's voice actresses implored viewers to forget that the episode had ever existed. There is a reason those particular colors were used in the first place. Historian Spyros Papapetros provides some situational context:

As animation experts explained, similar visual techniques (called "paka-paka") had been repeatedly used in Japanese cartoons to cause a sense of tension. But in that particular segment the flashes, alternating in every second, were double the normal number, and combined with the intensity of the colors, the photo-stimulation became overbearing. Following the initial "Pokemon hysteria" in Japan, the incident sparked an international debate in newspapers and on the Internet between the enraged parents who criticized television executives and the enthusiastic teenagers who defended their favorite show (301).

There was already concern raised by parents and advocacy groups about the effects of violent cartoons on impressionable children, but the outcry over a scary foreign property was enough to make waves onto the rest of the American visual media landscape. It also convinced the general American public that cartoons, harmless as they looked, could, in fact, have tangible effects on children. The Pokémon incident went down in history as a painful reminder that "human subjects instinctively attribute agency to inanimate images and things when something bad is happening to them" (Papapetros 303). In other areas, the potential impact of animation onto viewers has been regarded more positively.

Nowhere is this clearer than in the Middle East, which is remarkable considering that there is a death of information related to animation of that region. "Historically," Van de Peer writes, "animation has been dominated by American or Asian producers and markets, but some animators...are starting to assert their Arab identity in their drawing styles and techniques" (158). Animation in the Middle East is a young medium with a young demographic and an entrepreneurial digital spirit that translates into financially viable projects, such as the collaboration with the French animation industry on the critically acclaimed Persepolis. The Middle Eastern animation industry is built around transnationalism, which is an attitude that "depends on the willingness of all subjects involved in the film experience" (Van de Peer 152). Despite how young animation is in the Middle East, its history goes back to the beginning of the twentieth century.

Since the 1930s, Middle Eastern animation has been dominated by Egypt. During World War II, the Egyptian ministry of defense utilized the Frenkel brothers' skills to create animated propaganda shorts to rally their people against the Nazis. The brothers' first film in 1939, National Defense, starred their human, camel-riding equivalent to Mickey Mouse as well as his girlfriend, who resembled an Egyptian Betty Boop. After that, the development of Middle Eastern animation has slowed down considerably due to high production costs and the need for skilled specialists, unavailable in the region until recently. The lack of infrastructure, funds and interest further complicated the already fraught relationship Arabs had with cinema and art. Van de Peer describes the root of such a troubled relationship:

Arab art focuses on portraying meaning and essence rather than representing the physical form of things. Decorative arts such as calligraphy, ceramics, architecture, and arts and crafts were far more acceptable than film or painting. There was and is a constant concern that the depiction of the moving human form comes too close to idolatry, as God is the only image-maker (Van de Peer 158).

Middle Eastern animated films heavily used allegories and non-linear structures in order to get around these restrictions, requiring the viewer to quietly question whatever social norms he or she has grown up with. In oppressive regimes such as those found in various parts of the Middle East, where political dissent is prohibited, these tactics are vital to subversion. Van de Peer thus succinctly summarizes how the Middle Eastern animation scene operates:

Animation can thus on the one hand indirectly criticize the political and social situation, and outwit the censor, as animals and children speak metaphorically about more pertinent situations. On the other hand, animation can draw attention directly to unspeakable situations that cannot be captured on film (159).

This type of underhanded subversion is not unlike how American animated shorts, particularly those starring the Warner Brothers' Looney Tunes, had to subtly work in their rebellious humor around the prohibitions of the Hays Code in the forties.

Animation collections document the same depth of cultural insight as other forms of archives. Unfortunately, the archival profession has not always used these collections in the best way. In the past, animated archival practices followed the "traditional process of stabilizing, organizing, and cataloging collections" which "may be an effective way to preserve content for posterity, but it is agonizingly slow, and has the effect of reducing access even further," (Jones 274). Timothy Jones, a researcher from the School of Film and Television Studies at the University of East Anglia, puts forth an example of the old-fashioned method as it fails to hold up for modern researchers as told by archivist Stephen Worth:

When you go to an archive you write down what you are looking for on a slip of paper and give it to the lady. After forty-five minutes she comes back and says: "here it is" or "we don't have that." It is like a big game of Go Fish. Instead of being a gatekeeper, the archivist should be an active promoter of the collection (274).

From Rebekah Taylor's perspective, the archives are often underutilized because "they tend to be isolated from the rest of the library" for secure, environmentally controlled storage (2). This practice could potentially prioritize preservation at the expense of accessibility.

Fortunately, several people have proposed ideas as to how animation archives can adapt to the modern era. According to Timothy Jones, "Archivists must accept new realities and adopt new technologies to bring communities into the archives to use it in new ways and allow it to thrive" (274). He brings up Rick Prelinger's model for the twenty-first century archive, which calls for archivists who prioritize access and act as spokespeople for their collections. The model is as follows:

The 21st century archive…must seek validation by creating abundance rather than maintaining scarcity. It must accept that archival ethics generally favor use over the fear of abuse. Above all, it needs to recognize that it is a cultural producer playing a primary role in the dissemination and exchange of images and sounds, not simply a wholesale repository relying on presenters, producers, and scholars to expose its treasures (Jones 274).

Jones then tackles the question: "Can the animation archive be a gathering space, a place where different users meet and engage in dialogue?" (274). He answers by putting a spotlight onto the International Animated Film Society (ASIFA) Hollywood Animation Archive in Burbank, California, as an example of how an archive uses digital technology to make the animation community's extensive historical heritage usable for artists today. ASIFA adapts by reforming education to nurture creative development, being designed as a "digital database," drawing inspiration from "the largest – albeit most transient – emergent archives, YouTube and even eBay," "ensuring unrestricted fair use from donors, and digitizes the collection," thus making it "possible to create an archive that may be explored without damage, and browse without a preconceived research agenda" and decontextualizing and making accessible "many decades of animation practice and change the very way the industry reproduces itself" (Jones 276, 278). This infrastructure is especially useful for accessing animated works made outside one's country of origin, since the majority of foreign animated works are unavailable for purchase and remain untranslated. On YouTube, users put up subtitled versions of various foreign shorts and animated films. If young animators have access to these different styles of animation, then this will result in a greater diversity of ideas and animation techniques.

 Meanwhile, Taylor has some ideas of her own. She claims that making animation archives more accessible entails turning them into more public-facing spaces like libraries. Taylor also recommends "running more events and workshops in archives, even if they are just for students and researchers" (9). One of her promotional documents describes how the UCA opens up its collections to their staff and students:

A number of pedagogical frameworks and activities have been developed to support object and archive-based learning, using archival materials for enhancing teaching, learning and research. Students can read, touch, browse, and feel the sketches, paintings, animation, press released (Lin & Taylor).

Being allowed to touch the archives is a major boon for increased access. After all, if students can go to college libraries and touch their rare books, then they can do the same to animated archives, provided they come in with gloves and clean hands. One case study, in which the purpose was to turn archive spaces into incubators for creative ideas, had the following results:

With archives and special collections for students in photography, in the form of a presentation, group work, and hands on session students were encouraged to discuss what they thought an archive was, how to find them, how it could be reused in their work, how archival cataloguing theory can be used with Photography narrative work, how you can look after your own work (Lin & Taylor).

Archival institutions could find a way to acquire foreign collections in addition to those of their home country and display them for students to see and feel. Infrastructure changes and increased outreach efforts will hopefully result in a more open and internationally minded animation community.

Works Cited

Blackledge, Olga. "Lev Kuleshov on Animation: Montaging the Image." Animation (17468477), vol. 12, no. 2, July 2017, p. 110. EBSCOhost, ezproxy.simmons.edu:2048/login?url=https://search-ebscohost-com.ezproxy.simmons.edu/login.aspx?direct=true&db=edb&AN=124050014&site=eds-live&scope=site.

Cook, Malcolm. "The Lightning Cartoon: Animation from Music Hall to Cinema." Early Popular Visual Culture, vol. 11, no. 3, n.d., pp. 237-254. EBSCOhost, ezproxy.simmons.edu:2048/login?url=https://search-ebscohost-com.ezproxy.simmons.edu/login.aspx?direct=true&db=edswah&AN=000323732500005&site=eds-live&scope=site.

Du, Daisy Yan. "Suspended Animation: The Wan Brothers and the (In)Animate Mainland-Hong Kong Encounter, 1947–1956." Journal of Chinese Cinemas, vol. 11, no. 2, June 2017, p. 140. EBSCOhost, ezproxy.simmons.edu:2048/login?url=https://search-ebscohost-com.ezproxy.simmons.edu/login.aspx?direct=true&db=edb&AN=123434398&site=eds-live&scope=site.

Jones, Timothy. "Animating the Archive: A Role for Creative Practice in the Animation Archive." Animation Practice, Process & Production, vol. 1, no. 2, 2012, pp. 273–283., doi:10.1386/ap3.1.2.273_1.

Krishnan, Shweta, et al. "From Unwanted Pregnancy to Safe Abortion: Sharing Information about Abortion in Asia through Animation." Reproductive Health Matters, vol. 23, no. 45, n.d., pp. 126-135. EBSCOhost, ezproxy.simmons.edu:2048/login?url=https://search-ebscohost-com.ezproxy.simmons.edu/login.aspx?direct=true&db=edswss&AN=000370882000014&site=eds-live&scope=site.

Lin, Yuwei and Taylor, Rebekah. Enterprising Archives for Object & Archive-based Learning in Arts and Media. In: Higher Education Entrepreneurship Group (HEEG) annual conference, 17-18 June 2014, Kingston University.

Papapetros, Spyros. "In/Animate Victims: Cultural Reactions to Animation." Communication & Critical/Cultural Studies, vol. 9, no. 3, Sept. 2012, pp. 300-306. EBSCOhost, doi:10.1080/14791420.2012.708973.

Taylor, Rebekah. Animation Archives: Collaboration with Archivists, Academics, and Practitioners. In: Society for Cinema and Media Studies (SCMS) Annual Conference, 25 - 29 March 2015, Montreal, Canada.

Taylor, Rebekah. Archiving a Feminist Animation Archive. In: Archiving Women in Film & TV Workshop, 14 May 2015, Brotherton Library, University of Leeds.

Van de Peer, Stefanie. "Fragments of War and Animation: Dahna Abourahme's Kingdom of Women and Soudade Kaadan's Damascus Roofs: Tales of Paradise." Middle East Journal of Culture & Communication, vol. 6, no. 2, Apr. 2013, pp. 151-177. EBSCOhost, doi:10.1163/18739865-00602003.

Wells, Paul. "Validating the Animated Film: Toys Stories, Trade Tattoos and Taiwan Tigers: Or What's Animation Ever Done for Us?" Themanummer Animatie, Tijdschrift voor Mediageschiedenis (Journal for Media History), vol. 15, no. 1, 2012, pp.5-24.

OTHER ARTICLES

FROM RELIGION TO POLITICS: THE DE FACTO POWER OF A SUFI BROTHERHOOD IN CYRENAICA

BY DIEGO LAUDATO

Introduction

This essay investigates the emergence and the evolution of a specific group of power in a remote region of Northern African: The Libyan Cyrenaica. The spatial framework is set between the Thirties of the 19th and the Thirties of the 20th centuries. In the last part of those years, this region was subjected to a colonial expedition from an European Country. Libya, indeed, was invaded by Italian armies in 1911. There, in addition to the troops of the Ottoman Empire, ruling power of the region, the colonizers faced the rebellion of the Bedouins tribes, organized under the flag of a religious brotherhood, the Sanusiya, which is the subject of this article. Born as a Sufi order, the Sanusiya became the main actor of Libyan resistance in Cyrenaica, keeping it in a permanent state of resistance from 1911 to 1933 against a foreign, unfaithful, invader.

Aim of this paper is to illustrate the socio-political role held by the Sanusi Brothers in that region. In particular, it will follow the switch that it had from a typical religious organization, included in the spiritual tradition of the area, toward a proper political actor. It will investigate the reasons and the ways through which it developed this powerful influence among the Bedouin tribes. In particular, it will be focused on the social services provided by the Order to the tribesmen, showing how and why the Ottoman Empire lacked this function. Because of this lack, actually, Sanusiya was able to insert itself in the local tribal system, becoming an element of unification of all its segments. This feature allowed a previous religious group to become a proper political representative for the Cyrenaican tribe. It became the only spokesman which could deal with the Ottoman Empire for the issues related to the Bedouins. Then, when the Italians arrived, it was the last bastion in the colonial struggle against an European State. Eventually, it will be shown how this link would survive even after the physical destruction of the Order.

The emergence of a Sufi Brotherhood in Cyrenaica

Defining Sufismis a very hard task. Actually, the debate about the meaning of this term, as well as

"

for many other important categories in Islamic studies, is still today open and wide. Through this umbrella expression every author could refer to whatever was useful for his own purpose. The history of the historiography is full of reference to very different definitions of the concept of Sufism[1]. Each meaning, of course, is deeply influenced by the specific context in which authors experienced their relation with Sufism it- self. The lack of a single definition led even many Sufi masters to refrain from using the concept of Sufism as a sharp category. Many Sufi experience have been therefore depicted as a unique, distinct from all the other ones. In other words, the concept of Sufism has a different value in every single manifestation in which it appears[2].

Perhaps it is possible to give a common definition starting from a very typical criticism about this concept: the issue about its translations. Shared opinion about the origin of the term Sufism refers to the Arab word ta- sawwuf, generally translated as "Islam Mysticism". However, this meaning has been largely contested by post-colonial scholars[3]. According to them, indeed, the notion of mysticism is too much informed by its Christian declination. They argued that the translation "Islamic Mysticism" is nothing more than a strained "orientalization" [4]. Nevertheless, from the Arab and even from the very Sufi environment, in recent times the term tasawwuf has been reproposed again in its English meaning of "mysticism" . In particular, the Sufi intellectual Abu l-Taftazani suggested that tasawwuf should be used as a category opened to a wider understanding of mysticism, including those experience out of the Islamic spirituality[5]. This idea finds an echo in the researches of another scholar of Islamic studies, Sara Sviri. She argued that rather than debate about the usefulness to find better translation, it could be rather more purposeful to enlarge the understanding of the notion of "mysticism" itself. She actually gave her own definition of it, stated as:

a current within religions and cultures associated with voluntary efforts aimed at gaining an intensified experience of the sacred[6].

This particular conception of the relation tasawwuf -"mysticism" actually allows to shape a more comprehensive and general category to which each particular Sufi experience, with its own whole of peculiar features, can be connected. Nowadays, this recent conception has been largely accepted and a group of scholars are applying the definition of Sufism as "Islamic Mysticism" in this wider sense[7].

Once given the definition of Sufism as an intensified experience of the Islamic spirituality, we can move on the focus of the article. The Sanusiya is a Sufi Brotherhood, or Order[8], developed in Cyrenaica starting from 1837. In relation with other Sufi Orders, the Sanusi of Cyrenaica were very rigorous in their orthodoxy, conforming their behaviors on the original teachings preached by Prophet Muhammad to the Bedouins in the 7th century, assuming that the lifestyle of those who lived in the 19th should had been the same of their ancestors[9]. Sanusiya's founder was al-Sanusi al-Kabir or, then known as the Grand Sanusi. He was born in Algeria in 1787, showing since his youth particular intelligence, piety and great ability in learning. He started his studies in his motherland and then he moved to an important school in Fez, Morocco, achieving the typical studies for a Muslim student of the time. From this moment, he started several pilgrimages, during which he preached and gathered the first disciples. He stayed in Hijax for six years, studying under Shaikhs in Mecca and al-Madina. He decided to follow in Yaman his most influential master, Sayyid Ahmad bin Idris al-Fasi, who had a struggle with a religious group in Mecca. At his master's death, the future Grand Sanusi created his own Order, namely the Sanusiya, set originally near Mecca, at Mt. Abu Qubais, in 1837[10].

The Sanusi Brotherhood soon achieved great success among the Bedouins of the Hijaz. According to this, it soon alarmed the Mecca's religious authorities. Because of this opposition, the Head of the Order followed his master's example, leaving the region. During the journey, he spent his time preaching among the Bedouins of the oases, instructing their faith. He reached firstly Tripoli, then Cairo. He eventually decided to move to Banghazi, in Libya, because the French colonial army in the meanwhile invaded Algeria. In 1843, he founded there what later would became the Mother Lodge of the Order, placed in al-Zawiyaal al-Baida, in Cyrenaica.   Nevertheless, he moved again to Mecca, leaving the Sanusi of Cyrenaica growing up without his direct guide. When he came back to the region, he set a new pole for the Order at Jaghbub, a very harsh oasis due to its geographical and atmospheric conditions. On the other hand, however, the new place was a very strategic spot from the political point of view. It was indeed out of the control of both the French and the Turkish governments. Moreover, it was set in a very central position in reference to the lodges[11] that in the meanwhile have been built in Cyrenaica, Tripolitania, Egypt and Sudan[12].

Electing Jaghbub as the new centre of the Sanusiya, the Grand Sanusi made a strategical choice for the Order: he oriented its missionary activity south- wards, looking at the heathen and semi-heathen inhabitants of the Sahara. From there, thus, he was also able to intercept the trade routes linking the desert to the Mediterranean Sea. Very soon, Sanusiya's lodges became fundamental spots for Bedouins's caravans, putting these tribes in contact with the Order'sfaith[13].

The de facto power of Sanusiya in Cyrenaica under the Turkish Administration

The Grand Sanusi was therefore able to gather new disciples among the Bedouins met on the caravan routes between the Sahara and the Mediterranean Sea. Through this expedient, in few time Order incredibly increased his members.

Cyrenaican Bedouins were Muslims. Since they lived far away from the core of Islam though they developed peculiar features for their spirituality which can be considered not strictly Islamic. In particular, they were devotees of saints, which is not something generally allowed to Muslims.

These saints have been called in European accounts Marabouts, translating the Arab term of Marabtin, (sing) Marabat[14]. Local tribesmen were very familiar with the Marabouts tradition, much more than with the legacy of the Sufi orders. Because of this, when the Grand Sanusi arrived in Cyrenaica, he was accepted as a Marabout, rather than a Sufi Shaikh. He was perceived as a man able to carry out miracles thanks to his baraqa, a flow of God's grace which springs from him toward surrounding people. His successors would inherited his baraqa, keeping his sanctity and, therefore, his authority. He would be buried in a shining shrine and adored as perhaps the most important, but still one among other adored Marabouts of Cyrenaica[15]. This tradition was at the basis of the Grand Sanusi's success. Because of the already established Marabout tradition, the Bedouins were willing to recognize his claimed religious legitimacy[16].

In its first phase, the Order was a missionary organization composed by people considered foreigners among Bedouins. Those who followed the Grand Sanusi in Cyrenaica from his previous pilgrimages were people with different backgrounds and lifestyle, with no kinship in the local tribal system. The center itself, Jaghbub, strategical for already shown reasons, was though out of any tribe's influence and therefore it prevented Sanusiya to be associated with a specific tribe[17]. The Order had a wide expansionist phase with Grand Sanusi's successor, his son Sayyid Muhammad al-Madhi. His missionary targets were still the heathen and semi-heathen population of the Sahara and in particular of Sudan. Since it was growing very quickly, the Order, and the whole of trading activities which it intercepted moving along the trade routes, required a different organization. Sayyid al-Madhi decided to move the capital to the Kufra oasis, a key meeting point for several desert courses. He transformed that place in a great emporium, becoming an inviting stop for caravans[18].

What eventually allowed the Brotherhood to achieve such influential role in the region was actually the attachment that tribes developed with the lodge built in their territory. Thezawiya generally worked in this way. It was held by a local Shaikh, loyal representative of the Head of the Order locally. Through the Shaikh's administration over the territory of the lodge, the influence of the Sanusiya was felt day by day by the local population. The Brothers were indeed used to carry out fundamental functions for the people's daily survival, fostering in this way the lodge's authority in the area. The Order was able to provide key social services to the Bedouin tribes, which the official ruling power, the Ottoman Empire, instead did not offer. The transformation of the Kufra oasis is a perfect example of what Sanusyia did for Bedouins. There as elsewhere, the Brotherhood provided both security for the trades and hospitality for local tribes. Another important role supplied by the Shaikhs was the arbiter for juridical disputes among Bedouins in conflict. Eventually, they also served as teachers for children[19]. In other words, every lodge acquired soon a much wider function than just a religious center. They could be used as schools, courts, defensive forts, commercial centers and even storehouses. Just keep in mind that the Sanusi's organization in lodges was an anomaly compared to the nomadic lifestyle of the Bedouins. They were used to cultivate the plot of lands around the lodge, storing the surplus and providing it to the moving caravans during their trade journeys. The Shaikhs were the pole of these functions, but several minor officials contributed to the social machine organized by the Sanusi [20].

One of the most important services provided by the local masters was the function of intermediary between the tribes and the Turkish administration. This actually suggests that the Ottoman Empire recognized, if not officially, the de facto power of the Sanusi brothers. In order to deal with the Bedouins for governmental issues, mostly related to taxation[21]. Turkish officials recognized the Shaikh's influence over Bedouins. This opens to a consideration about spheres of influence and the power relations emerging between an official ruler detached from its periphery and a parallel power arose among the society. The Sanusiya was almost completely a tribal phenomenon. North African cities hosted very few zawiya. In the urban context, indeed, Turkish administration was more capable to achieve its social duties[22]. The Cyrenaican social environment, instead, presented a major nomadic component, i.e. the Bedouins. The Turks achieved to set their power in the cities, easily dealing with the peasantry, geographically fixed on the same territory. In the urban environment, under its conditions, the ruling power could easier provide those social services which instead lacked among the nomads. Cyrenaican Bedouins, on the contrary, were always in movement, frustrating the Empire's ambition of a direct grip over the tribes. Turkish officials tried to influence the tribal elements closer to the cities. The linking bridge they found was the local Sanusi representative. The Order, through its local Shaikhs, was actually involved by the Sultan's officials in all those decision related to the Bedouin tribes set on the territory. In this way, the " Sublime Porte" recognized the former's authority over the latter[23]. At the heyday of their success, actually, the most important Sanusi families were respected and esteemed by the Turks, which carefully did not encroach their de facto power among the tribesmen[24].

As matter of facts, Turks were not so much interested in what happened in this region. Libya was a very peripheral region of the Empire, which was actually concerned by both internal and external crisis. In particular Cyrenaica was a very poor territory, from which it was almost impossible to gain profits. Therefore, their interventions were basically limited to sanction the sacred authority of the Sultan and to benefit of a working tax system. All the other functions generally performed by a government were practically delegated to Sanusiya. The Order actually plunged the roots of its success exactly on these social services: education, justice, security[25]. It was nothing but a political compromise, based on the reality. The Turks, because of both the unwillingness and the impossibility to establish a direct dominion in Cyrenaica, recognized the de facto power of the Sanusi Brothers. The Order, on the other hand, understood that this role in-between two pre-existing actors could reinforce its influence. Actually, this prediction was correct. The Bedouins found in the Brotherhood a recognized institution through which dealing with the Turks. For the first time in their history, the tribes started to see themselves as a single political whole, a sort of proto-nation that had its representative in the Order[26].

The Italo-Sanusi Wars

On October 1911 Italy started its colonial expedition in Libya. When the Italians arrived in the country, they found almost zero resistance from the Ottomans. The latter were experiencing indeed both an inner political crisis, due to the Young Turks[27] revolution occurring in those same years, and an assault on its much more strategical dominions in the Balkan peninsula. The Turkish armies, split on different fronts and halved by inner conflicts, were therefore not able to provide a successful defense of the Libyan territory. The last bastion against the final conquest from a Christian, European, colonial invader eventually became the Sanusiya.

In Cyrenaica Italians made some tactical mistakes. Next to the pure military ones, they confused the Bedouins attitude towards the Turks. They assumed that il famoso papa nero[28] was trying to found his own independent kingdom in the region and therefore his most fierce enemy should necessarily be the Ottoman Sultan[29]. This already arguable belief did not take in account that for a Muslim religious brotherhood the idea to be governed by a Christian, stranger power was nothing but unacceptable. In reality, it has been already noted how the Sanusi and the Turks established a political compromise that, given some taxation's struggles and other kind of minor quarrels, worked almost peacefully[30]

In the perspective of a Western country, one needed condition to set warfare in the proper way was to face an equivalent institution. When the Ottoman Empire withdrew from Cyrenaica, they represented no longer a valid representative for diplomatic relations. Sanusiya, because of the reasons which has been explicated before, emerged therefore as the best standard which could gather together the Bedouins against the foreign enemy. Once forced to face an outside element opposed to it, the local system of tribes felt the need to unify all its segments in a single unity. On the other hand, how- ever, they did not feel the need to affirm themselves as an official political authority as it could be defined in a Western perspective. Such switch was actually achieved exactly through through the diplomatic process started by the Italians. Turkish armies rapidly withdrew and a peace treaty was signed between the Italian King and the Sultan. However, in Cyrenaica the war went on and the resistance reorganized itself under the banner of the Order. Italian diplomats soon recognized the de facto power of the Sanusi, but it was not enough. In order to impose their authority on the local population, Italians were interested in to coming to terms with the Bedouins. The former though did not accept to deal with a disconnected whole of tribes. Therefore, the Italians fell in the contradictions that, in order to affirm their own authority on a specific territory, they needed to promote the local power, i.e. the Brothers, to an equivalent actor which fit in the Western international law[31].

It seemed that the Order willingly accepted this new role. It started to claim the status of proper political organization. Major acknowledgments arrived by those Turkish troops that remained in the region as sort of mercenaries, enlarging the resistance ranks. Enver Bey[32]. leader of the Turkish army in loco, flew away in order to fight for the Sultan in the First Balkan War. Be- fore to leave the country, however, he decided to visit the Head of the Order at Jaghbub. During his visit, it seemed that he asked the Brothers to carry on the resistance against the Italians as the Sultan's representative. Given this symbolic ratification, from that moment on the Sanusi started to define themselves as the "al-Hakumaal-Sanusiya", the Sanusiya Government [33].

For this paper's purposes, a proper account of the war is not needed. Thanks to the switch achieved by the Order, the struggle started to be called the Italo-Sanusi War, and no longer the Italo-Turkish one, as it officially started. The Sanusiya, pushed by external reasons, ceased to be associated as a religious institution, or at least was no longer just one of them, becoming a proper political organization [34]. The war ended its first phase in 1917, then it started again in 1923, lasting until 1932. If the first one started as a war against the Turks and then slowly switch toward a war against the Order, the Second Italo-Sanusi War started already against the Brothers and the population that at that time they officially represented.

Fascist were aware that the Order had the value to transform the typical resistance of a native people against a Western colonizer in a religious and national struggle for the safeguard of their own independence. Because of this reason, Sanusiya achieved a timeless, honorable place in the hearts of Cyrenaican people[35]. Fascists could not accept the constant presence of an alternative power in a land that they were trying to promote as the pillar of a renewed Roman Empire. Therefore, they tried to eradicate this link between the populations and the Brothers. Every local zawiya, was confiscated or destroyed. This goal was perceived as the final act in the extirpation process of the Sanusi Order from Cyrenaica[36].

Conclusion

After nine years of bloody war, on the 24 January 1932 Cyrenaica officially became a calmed down country, under the colonial rule of the Italians. The conquest required an overwhelming effort for the Italian State, as pointed out by Benito Mussolini himself, who wrote: Cirenaica verde di piante ´e diventata rossa di sangue[37]. Eventually, the Sanusiya was wiped out by the region, after it represented the de facto power there for more than an half-century. It was born as a Sufi order founded by an Algerian Shaikh in 1837, initially welcomed by the local population as one among others Marabouts. The Grand Sanusi, however, was able to distinguish himself from other previous "saints" thanks to his pronounced strategical sense. He set his missionary activity in the midst of the trade routes between the Sahara region and the Mediterranean Sea, gathering his disciples among the heathen and semi-heathen tribes of Bedouins. Intercepting the tribal sys- tem, the Sanusi Brothers starting very soon to provide it of social services which the ruling power, the Turkish Administration, was not able to offer. The latter, actually, in the very same time was shaken by both internal and external struggles, which basically took away its concern from a peripheral and poor area like Cyrenaica. In this way, in very few years the Brotherhood was able to establish its de facto power among the local Bedouins, signing an unofficial compromise with the Turks to divide the respective sphere of influence in the region. The Italians' arrival altered this working pact. From one side, it pushed the segmented Bedouin tribes to form a proper coalition under the flag of its most representative spokesman, the Order. From the other hand, thus, the fast withdrawal of the Turkish armies forced the Italian diplomats to find a new political element which could represented an equivalent in the needed negotiations. This process strengthened even more the link between the tribes and Sanusiya, which more and more transformed the resistance of a native people in a religious and national struggle. When Fascists decided that an unsolved conflict in Northern Africa was too much embarrassing for their imperial ambitions, they started a systematic process of devastation, violating previous treaties and destroying casualness tens of thousands of people.

The Order continued its valorous resistance until its final destruction. How- ever, the link established between the Cyrenaican population and the Sanusi Brothers lasted. To understand how deep this tie was, one should look at the choice of the first King of the newborn Libyan State in 1951. When the United Nations' General Assembly transformed the country in an autonomous state, indeed, they choose the last Head of the Sanusi Brothers: Idris bin Muhammad al-Madhi as-Senusi. He was clearly chosen because of his friendship with the British government, which he deepened during his exile in Egypt during the Second Italo-Sanusi War. However other reasons contributed. Idris I of Libya represented indeed a King liked by the international community, and at the meanwhile beloved by a population who saw him as the last bastion in the fight for their independence.

Through his crowning, the great political role that the Sanusiya achieved in the previous century, firstly in Cyrenaica and then for the whole Libya, was definitely sanctioned.

References

[1] G. Cecere, The Shaykh and the Others. Sufi perspectives on Jews and Christians in Late Ayyubid and Early Mamluk Egypt, in Entangled Religions. Interdisciplinary Journal for the Study of Religious Contact and Transfer , 6,1, 2018, pp. 34-94.

[2] E.E. Evans-Pritchard, The Sanusi of Cyrenaica, Clarendom Press, Oxford, 1954.

[3] N. Hofer, The Popularisation of Sufism in Ayyubid and Mamluk Egypt, 1173-1325, Edinburgh University Press, Edinburgh, 2015.

[4] A. Knysh, Historiography of Sufi Studies in the West and in Russia, in Written Monuments of the Orient , 1, 4, 2006, pp- 206-238.

[5] M. Le Gall, The Ottoman Government and the Sanusiyya: a Reappraisal, in J. Middle East Stud. 21 (1989), USA, pp. 91-106.

[6] B. Mussolini, Introduction, in: A. Teruzzi, Cirenaica Verde, Mondadori, Milano,1931.

[7] A. Prosperi, G. Zagrebelsky, P. Viola, M. Battini, Storia e identit´a 3. Il Novecento e oggi, Einaudi Scuola, 2012.

[8] E. Said, Orientalism, Pantheon Books, United State, 1978.

[9] S. Sviri, Sufism: Reconsidering Terms, Definitions and Processes in the Formative Period of Islamic Mysticism, in Les maitres soufis et leur disciples: iii-v siecle de l'hegire (ix, xi s.). Enseignement, formation et transmission, pp. 17-13, ed. by G. Gobillot,J.J. Thibon, Beirut, 2012.

[10] Abu I-Taftazani, Al-turuq al-sufiyya fi Misr. (Rasa'il al-Majlis al-a'la' lil-turuq al-sufiyya 2).Cairo: Matba' at al-Amaniyya.

THE THREE LIVES OF THE DINGO: AN ANALYSIS OF THE AUSTRALIAN NATIVE DOG

BY MARICA FELICI

Introduction

«It is the colouring that strikes you first. In a pale and sparse land which at dusk can turn to an intense chrome yellow, he looks luminous, almost unreal»

(May 1986:8)

Dingoes are iconic Australian animals, like kangaroos and koalas. We can find dingos on postcards, as characters in children's books, and presented as one of the main attraction in organized-tours for tourists, for example on Fraser Island (Queensland) that is part of the Great Sandy National Park, where dingoes live freely. Nonetheless, dingo's perception in present-day Australia is typify as "dual", being simultaneously a cunning wolf and a friendly dog, an animal that needs to be eradicated (for its predatory role towards sheep and cows) but also protected (as an Australian "native" species, endangered by hybridization with domestic dogs and by mass killings). The dualism that surrounds the image of the dingo has a long history, with roots in the Dreaming, the aboriginal myth about life and death, and in the ways European settlers had signified their encounter and their lives with this animal.

Even though the dingo is considered a native Australian animal, it is not. Studies are still producing new information, but thanks to archaeological research and analysis of dingo's mitochondrial DNA there is a general agreement among scholars about the fact that dingoes were introduced in Australia in the late Holocene era, more likely not before 4000 years ago. A question now arises: where dingoes come from? Again, there is more to discover, but researchers agree on South East Asia as the place from where dingoes arrived in Australia. Dr Melanie Fillios, a researcher from University of New England (Australia), and Paul Taçon, professor at Griffith University (Australia), suggested that dingoes are likely to have been introduced to Australia by Toalean hunter-gather peoples from South Sulawesi in Indonesia, perhaps after obtaining them from people in Borneo.

Given the fact that there is no evidence that a land bridge connection ever existed between South East Asia and Australia, therefore dingoes must have arrived with the company of humans via sea. What is particularly interesting is that there is an aboriginal myth which might confirm the aforementioned hypothesis about the arrival of the dingo in Australia: the myth speaks about a dingo jumping off a boat and running into the bush (Parker 2006:5). This myth is performed during the corroboree, a ceremony in which through singing and dancing Australian aboriginals recalled and recreate the Dreaming. This myth also tells us that dingoes had found a specific place in the lives of aboriginal peoples, both in the mythological and supernatural realm and in the practical life.

The Dreaming Dingo

«When Aboriginal man goes through the law he might become [...] a dog man.
Those dingoes watch over the dog man [...].
They do their job – they are part of our Dreaming»
(an Antikarinya Aboriginal elder in Burdon 2017:64-65)

Australia is a large continent peopled by a multitude of Aborigines groups which differs from each other in terms of languages and cultures. As a consequence, the way in which dingoes are represented in native Australians imagination varied; notwithstanding, it appears that soon after their arrival in Australia, Aboriginals incorporated dingoes into their lives and their mythological system, with some similarities among the different groups. In particular, scholars agree in underlining that the dingo plays an important role in The Dreaming. Rose (1992:43,44) states that the term "Dreaming" is used by natives Australians to indicate «a wide range of concepts and entities», and that they prefer to use instead the wording 'The Law' (Rose 1994; Stockton 2000). The term "Dreaming" as a matter of fact is the wrong translation given by the colonizers of an Arrente phrase that can, as Stockton (2000:149) suggests, be better translate as "originating from eternity". This way of naming the aboriginal cosmogony seems to be in agreement with what "The Law" means: in Stanner's words (1979:24) it is «a sacred, heroic time long ago when men and nature came to be as they are; [...] One cannot "fix" The Dreaming in time: it was, and it is, everywhen... [...]».Stanner also states that «[t]he Dreaming is many things in one» (1979:24): in fact, it is a "map" that Aboriginal people used, and still use, to orientate themselves on how to properly behave towards other living things and the environment; but it is also a cosmogony, that is the myth of primordial creation. In this sense, The Dreaming is when the ancestral spirits were shaping the land and other living beings as they are now. «Boundaries between species, expressed as shape, colour, behavior, and habitat are an example of conditions determined in Dreaming. [...] Many animals now have characteristics they acquired when they were Dreaming» (Rose 1992: 45). Among those animals, there is an exception: the dingo. The dingo is one of the "ancestral spirit" that created the land and its inhabitants that still walk the Land it used to do in the Dreamtime. Among the Yarralin people, a community in the North Territory, studied by Deborah Bird Rose (1994), there is the belief that dingoes created humans in term of shaping their external appearance. Not only life, but human death too was originated by the dingo. There are several myths describing the Moon giving the Dreaming Dingo the opportunity to gain eternal life, and the dingo always losing it. Rose (1994) reports a story from the Victoria River District in the Northen Territory: the Moon wanted to contract a marriage against the Law with him mother-in-law; as a consequence, a big argument arose between him and all the animals/people. The verbal fight between Moon and Dreaming Dingo ended with the permanent death of the second: the Moon offered Dreaming Dingo the possibility to return to life by drinking Moon's urine in order to share the same destiny; however, Dreaming Dingo refused, and when he was dead, he tried several times to come back to life but without success. «Trough the actions of dingo and moon, death became a fact of human existence» (Rose 1994:49).

The connection drawn in The Dreaming between humans and dingo is also explicated in myths about shape-shiftings; usually, there are human beings that for different reasons turn into dingoes. Shape-changing creatures are starred in a great number of myths, for instance in hunting myths. From these type of myths emerges a different image of the dingo: one in which it is a negative presence symbolizing wilderness. Parker (2006:181,182) reports the so-called myth "The Bora of Baiame": it is about a large group of shape-shifting ancestral spirits who reunites for a ceremony; among them, there are Dreaming Dingoes called Madhi. The dingoes misbehave during the ceremony making noise and not listening to the elders; as a punishment, they are forever deprived of the ability to speak human language.

As it has already been underlined, the dingo is an ancestral spirit that shapes the world and establishes the Law; it behaves at the same time as a creator and a destructor: the Dreaming Dingo breaks its own rule and acts like a trickster. Moreover, dogs/dingoes are depicted having negative or uncanny attributes, for example, they are disloyal and when a prey is captured, they do not share it with their masters. Kolig (1978) points out that Aboriginal myths are modeled on the basis of the observation of nature and its beings, and this is why the dingo emerges as a dualistic creature: it is brave and faithful, a great companion, as shown by the myth "Manindi, a special dingo", where a giant lizard threaten a native camp and the dingo Manindi kill the lizard to protect the people; but it is also a wild and blood-thirsty animal, dangerous for other mythical beings, as in a myth from Southern Kymberly reported by Kolig (1978:101) where two mythical dogs/dingoes run away from their master and kill two ancestral spirits in the form of emus; after the killing, they feed on the preys.

Overall, in the mythical knowledge the dingo play a dualistic role, representing good and positive behaviors, and bad and negative ones; both the creative dingo and the "wild dog" emerged from the observation of reality. On the one hand myths in which the dingo is characterized as a positive creature underline the unity and intrinsic connection between humans and canine animals; on the other hand, hunting and warning myths teach that dingoes can be "wild", and so can people: in this role the dingo represents for Aboriginal people «a powerful symbol for moderation in behavior» (McIntosh in Smith and Litchfield 2009:125), a way to identify a dangerous member of society. Quite interestingly, it is possible to find another narrative involving the dingo which representation matches to some extent the Aboriginal's one: the narrative forged by the European colonials.

The dingo in the colonial project

«I arrived in this country and found myself surrounded by objects as strange as if I had been
transported to another planet»
(Jonh Gould in Stuart 2013:27)

The conquest of Australia was born as a means to create a new place to send different categories of people who were considered to be social problems. The aim was to displace people and at the same time to control them. This "new" land became pretty soon the land of convicts, rural workers, and outlaws. The colonial project planned for Australia by the British Empire was one where the colony itself must be self-sufficient, thus trough exploration, settlement and development Australia was "discovered" and occupied. But controlling the land was not enough: there was the need to take control of the land from the people who already lived there. According to Rose (1994:9), the conquest of Australia was organized around two major strategies: killing and control. And for what native fauna is concerned, the second option seemed to be the only one applicable.

The first encounter between the dingo and Europeans happened when British colonizers established the colony of New South Wales. From this moment began a complicated and not devoid from contradictions relationship that was shaped at the beginning by the scientific "read" of the dingo. One of the first descriptions of the dingo is made by Captain Arthur Phillip, the commander of the First Fleet that arrived in Botany Bay in 1789. Governor Phillip was aware of the necessity of documented the natural history of the colony, especially for the possible benefit that new and in some extent "exotic" stuff could bring to the commerce of Great Britain. Among those exotic things, there was the dingo, that is called by Governor Phillip in his report "The Dog of New South Wales" (1789:174). Notwithstanding, one of the first things that he wrote down is« [it] (the dingo) has much of the manners of the dog, but is of very savage nature, and not likely to change in this particular» (1789:274). This description was attached to a portrait of a female specimen that was sent by the Governor as a gift to the Marchioness of Salisbury. Another specimen met the same fate, and was sent to Europe as a present; and again, the account underlines the ferocity of the animal, with the subsequent comment «it is scarcely to be expected that this elegant animal will ever become familiar» (1789:275). Nevertheless, several attempts of own dingoes as pets were made from the colonial elite as a consequence of the fact that dingoes were associated with dogs. But the one with the dogs was not the only association that has been made: from the earliest days of the colonization, the dingo was described with lupine characteristics. As more accounts and observations were recorded during the early days of settlements in Australia, the dingo was always described as a lupine figure; these type of descriptions became even more frequent when the dingo was target as a "native enemy" by the settlers, that is when in the XIX century the sheep industry was established.

The importance of the sheep industry is crucial to understanding the depiction of the dingo as a vermin by the colonizers: the sheep industry from being a pillar of the success of the colonial project became one of the cores of the newly Euro-Australian identity. It is out of doubt that dingoes injured and killed sheet stock, and from farmers' accounts it is evident that dingoes kill in excess of their food-related needs; nonetheless, the dingo was depicted as a murderous pest that kill sheep almost consciously. In fact, the dingo is usually described in the colonial discourse as "canning". While the domestic dogs worked with the farmers, helping them controlling the livestock, the dingo played against them, mass-killing the sheep in sneaky and deceitful manners. Representations of the dingo as cunning were easily traced by the colonists having in mind two points: the first one is the observation of the dingo's behavior as Corbett (in Parker 2006:26) claims. The second reason why the dingo is described as cunning comes from the association made by the European between the dingo itself and the wolf.

The experience at the base of this interpretation of the dingo derived from the Europeans' experience with the American wolf depicted as misleading the shepherds and their dogs. Moreover like the wolf, the dingo possesses the power of reasoning, a power that in the colonial discourse is seen as being used by the wolf/dingo to reach their goal that is, of course, killing the sheep. The "war" set in place by the farmers against the dingo was perceived as natural and rightful because of the similarity between the dingo itself and the American wolf; in fact, wolves were «routinely killed by park rangers in American National Parks during the early years of the twentieth century» (Parker 2006:29). By killing sheep, dingoes were acting against the farmers and were threatening the success of the colonial project; as a consequence, they began to be seen as vermin. Farmers set traps, they used poisons (as the strychnine) against dingoes and they hunted dingoes down on horseback; soon enough, the colonial governments established a bounty for each dingo pelt delivered, pushing even more the practice of dingo shooting especially because trapping dingoes with high bounties on them was seen as a source of esteem. Notwithstanding, the problem represented by dingoes attacks on sheep was not solved; at this point, the single farms began to fence their own properties until this method developed into an actual fence long 5,309 kilometers and nearly two meters high that goes from South Australia, through New South Wales and ends in Queensland. This barrier is known as the "Great Dingo Fence" and it had come into place over many decades; it was built with the purpose of separate the sheep from the dingoes. But not only the fence was not that effective given the fact that dingoes could slip through it (while other animals, such as kangaroos, were "trapped" in it while jumping on the other side), it is also the longest barrier ever created by humans against a perceived foe and with its presence «creates an odd dualism in the profound silence of the Outback Australia where "this side" and "the other side" assume tantalising connotations» (May 1986:59). These two sides are respectively the farmers lands, which importance lies not merely in its economic values but mostly in in the fact that it symbolizes the "civilized garden", a place familiar and not touched by chaos; and the "bush", the wilderness that held a peculiar position in the colonial's minds because it represents something entirely unknown that is dreadful, but fascinating at the same time. Furthermore, the symbolic Great Fence were separating two more "others": the European colonizers and the Aboriginals.

As already mentioned, the dingo was inserted in a specific colonial discourse that denigrates and sketches it as a vermin worth to die; the same colonial discourse involves Aboriginal people. The settlement of Australia by Europeans was based on the doctrine of terra nullius, the idea that the Australian land was empty and unowned by people; as a consequence, Aboriginal presence undermined this "rightful" occupation by settlers. Aborigines were forced out of their territories likewise the dingoes were outcasted from the farm areas. Aborigines went back to their lands every night in search for food and water (Parker 2006:19), and dingoes ventured "on the other side of the fence" to feed on sheep and cows. Human and non-human natives were thus perceived as unwanted and both were inserted in a discourse that had the aim to justify the needs to eliminate them (and justification was particularly necessary for the eradication of the human natives given the fact that, after all, they were human beings).

The dingo and the Aborigines became part of a denigratory discourse built upon a narrative that describes both of them as cunning and treacherous. The category of "cunning" applied to the dingo has already been discussed; for what concerns its application to the Aborigines this

category, rather than the one of "cleverness", was used by settlers to represent the mental capacities of Aboriginal people: «the settlers "were forced" to admit the skill of the Aboriginal fighters, but they chose words which evoked betrayal rather than skill. Using descriptions related to animal instincts rather than higher logic, they slanted praise into denigration» (Parker 2006:27). Placing native Australians in an intellectual and moral inferior position and tracing a parallel between them and the dingo, already characterized as worth to die, was the tool used by colonizers to justify acts of aggression towards them and their removal from the lands. As Parker (2006) highlights, in colonial culture the analogy between humans and animals was seen as shameful, and dingo discourse was used to denigrate humans as well as dingoes. Quite interestingly, the same dingo discourse of colonial birth is still influential today, and it is still applied to the public perception of the dingo and on its treatment.

In which "side of the fence" the dingo stands today?

«The challenge will be to conceive gardens without fence»
(Instone 1998:464)

This phrase accurately describes the contemporary issues regarding the strategies applied to manage the dingo and that these strategies do not work perfectly. Today's perception of the dingo in contemporary Australia is quite different from the one of colonial times, but still dualistic and still complicated. The main shift that occurred is that now the dingo is seen as a native Australian animal: the Canis lupus dingo was officially adopted as "pure-breed" Australian in 1993 (Smith 1999:299), and it is now referred to as "wild Australian dog". This new status had the aim to acknowledge the rightful presence of the dingo in Australia, but influential dualistic discourses are in place and they lead to different attitudes towards the treatment of the dingo that can be called "the cull or the cuddle". At the foundation of the "cuddle" strategy there is a new romanticized image of the dingo, while "the cull" one is based on the vision of the dingo as wild and as a threat for the well-being of humans (and, again, of sheep). The romantic version of the dingo goes hand in hand with the revaluation of the (American) wolf that is now perceived as "noble and wise" (Parker 2006:234); the dingo was characterized in the same way in the Dreaming and such representations, in addition to the contemporary «anthropocentric in reverse» (Parker 2006:240), that is the idea that animals are better then humans, are utilized by non-indigenous Australians to shape a new discourse around the dingo that on one hand lead to the protection of the dingo in National Parks, and on the other is used to promote a specific type of tourism. These two aspects intersect in Fraser Island, an island located along the southeastern coast of the state of Queensland, and that is a part of the Great Sandy National Park. The island's environment is protected, and from it derives a view of the island as a pristine place where it is possible to come into contact with wild animals. This characteristic lead to the development of the island of the so-called "ecotourism", «the popular habit of holidaying into the wilderness» (Parker 2006:244). One of the main elements used to promote ecotourism on Fraser Island are dingoes proposed the epitome of wilderness, and this proposal works because they are in fact pretty rare in the sense that they are one of the last groups of "pure-breed" in Australia. Although these dingoes are considered worthy of care and protection, their increasing contacts with tourists result in a series of issues that leads to cull them. Dingoes on Fraser Island are grown accustomed to humans; as a consequence, they stay nearby the camping grounds in search for food (even because tourists sometimes feed them). It is possible to consider dingoes that frequent tourist areas as half-tamed and half-wild. But when the dingo "comes too close" and end to hurt someone, the tourists' expectations of the friendly dog living in a non-threatening wild paradise (as the tourist organization depicted it) are disillusioned. And when a dingo transpasses the boundaries of the places decided for them thus entering the ones reserved for humans, the dingo is shot dead by rangers, despite their status of protected animals within National Parks.

Conclusions

The dingo arrived in Australia approximately 4000 years ago and since then it has been surrounded by a multitude of different attitudes: the dingo moved from being considered as one of the makers of the Land and all its inhabitants when Australia was still in the hands of Aboriginal people, to be the quintessence of badness in its role of sheep killer in the colonial period. The characterization of the dingo both in Aboriginal mythology and in colonial discourse started from the observation of the natural behavior and physical appearance of this animal, but the animal that emerges from those representations is all but natural. «The colonisation of Australia involved the meeting of one culture that defined itself as absolutely different from animals, with another that defined itself as indistinguishable from animals» (Franklin in Stuart 2013:62): on the one hand the Aboriginal discourse propose a dingo that shares a position in the environment with them, a dingo "which belongs". On the other, the European settlers thought the environment to exists for human's well-being and thus whatever interfered with their exploitation of the colony had to be eliminated: Aborigines for not being worthy of occupying the land, and dingoes for their threat of one of the way in which settlers were using the Australian colony, that is the sheep industry.
In present-day Australia the dingo is still in the "hand" of humans, and depending on which discourse it is considered the dingo can be an iconic figure, a dangerous wild beast, or a "tricky" entity always ready to cross boundaries; thus the dingo is positioned in the realm of "belonging and not-belonging". «For Australia it [the dingo] provides a potent symbol for questioning where we draw the line between wilderness and civilization» (Instone 1998:458): this problematic question is still without answer, and for now the solution utilized to keep to a safe distance the

dingo is (again) a fence to which the Australian native dog is kept "on the other side".

POETRY

WELCOME TO YOUR OWN WORLD!

BY TRUPTI REKHA DASMAHAPATRA

O' Dear!
You have been unseen for a long time,
We yearn for your pleasant sounds;
Murmuring sounds of streams, sights of flying dove,
Pleasant jumps of dolphin, beautiful scene cloudy sky,
wild dance of waves, mild breeze, lovely care of you....

We have been a techno freaky,
Is that the reason you left us?
Or it's our fault?
Yeah, we pushed you out from your territory.

Taking out every part of you,
cutting trees, removing forests, modifying rivers,
To build a new world,
we have tortured you a lot,
We know your pain,
Still not able to mitigate it,
We have been rude to you,
To see a different world!

We ignored the old world,
welcome the new techy world,
But this different world pushed us to ocean of virus.

Self-quarantine taught us a great lesson,
We realized your value,
No mall, no theatre, no technology can replace you,
your care, your love, your gifts are irreplaceable.

We used to get self-healing from you,
but the new world takes us hospital each time,

We forgot the natural remedy
depending upon the new technology,
But today it failed to cure modern virus,
Natural remedy is only solution for it.

We have realized your sacrifice,
Started enjoying you as before,
Our hearty gratitude to you,
please come back to us,
Occupy your own territory.

A PLAGUE HARVEST

BY DAVE SIMONE

Verse 1

The crank rumbled in Tsona-speak.
Of plumbing soot and tinkers bleak.
Snaking farther into the endless smithy,
In the land of the undying Sun.
'Tis perilous scatters of Sarehole mill.
With the smoky eye patches and window teeth.
Clothed heat removes the brogues,
Not from my mission feet
But from the tongue of the native son.
The haze bears correctly the sounds of our name
The jay-train goes rogue
To the humour of the man within.
As the countryside wane

Verse 2

Shades of earth, darkness belly
Full bare, fuller hell, sheol's lot.
The vale that was Bathurst spit.
Air afoul, great spirits doth ail
Men as mounds, vile winds avail
Fetid breath and garments black
For even charon whose death ferry,
Reject these ones as souls far lost
There, arose nary who cried not sore
At Hansen's behest.

Verse 3

Mounds of earth, shadows of men about
In filthy raiments, they lay without.

Their infirmities they hide,
To slake the clean of their revile
Naaman's peril, this valley is heard,
Yon of Israel's foe, valiant on gruesome bane
Spat, mangled, unto help; all claws raising,
Sealed in a temple of rods unblest.

Verse 4

'This one, a shaman of the caves, a leader.
Liquid sores, gossamer scars
Bolus of head and mane,
No longer the crown to fit.
Misshappen nightmare with talons blunt,
Behind the veil, Montauk cut lips.
My nether churned in bitterest bile
And revulsion bade me no peace.
He lifted up his eyes unto the heavens
With his stringed beads to chant
For to rid him of his doom, his wounds pale,
As the Horseman he prayed to.

Verse 5

Through the looking glass, I canter
On steel hooves and coaches
Ere the night falls on the deep
One with the revelries of the outlawed
Marshalled unto weak armies.
In their wake, a threnode apiece,
The biers goes forever onwards
As the bards sings.

Verse 6

"One for the abbot who prims the flesh of the cleaned
And for the thankful hapful, that our Lord healed.

Two for those who sits outside Samaria gates
That makes enemies mishear sounds of gallantry.
Nine for the harvest of cleansed fools
Who knew not what it meant
To be rid of thee,
Oh bane of glorious Might.

GREAT WHITE SMOKE

BY H. L. RIVERS

Beat. Beat. Beat.
Holding my breath.
The calm before the storm.
The lightening, the thunder,
Their weapons are ideals
And scriptures from ancient texts.

Hatred and fear hail
All in the name of an
Old Testament God
Who has tied my hands and
Gagged my mouth.

Eyes. Blink. Eyes. Judge.
Is she racist? Does she self-hate?
Is she liberal? Is she straight?
Is she Christian? Or worse,
Agnostic, atheist?

Burn. Burn. Burn.
String her up!
Tie her to a stake,
Set her words alight
Drown her in smoke
Let her choke on her words!
Wait for her to beg and plead
Down on her knees where
She should always be,
But we will let her burn anyway.

Greedy flames
Taking bite after bite
Until there are no more
Words.
Only great white
Smoke.

MADNESS

BY NAIOMI LLOYD LEWIS

All Alice had to worry about was her cat.

Oh Dinah is such a dear darling thing!

Dinah darling, won't you fetch me a mouse for lunch?

Let's pursue the impossible,

Like Alice.

Six impossible things before lunch.

Shit! It's that time again, I must go.

Lunch for the babies.

Babies.

Out of the rabbit hole and into the oven.

SPIDERS HISTORY

BY NETA SHLAIN

Far back in the corner husky daddy's
weaving a basket of red and blue
into which he nearly falls
jumping through the hoops
hovering along the white wall
forgetting the befitting fable
for another day forged
in the corner palace.

Radio hammers louder than noise -
clanking cutlery and cups -
into coffee-cuddling customers
under the cover of a crowded curve.

Hold on, husky daddy, don't fall into that trap
trip up or drop onto the table
honestly. Tell them a tale
for history's sake, don't wait to be asked to
lie. You know better
than untangling the web
you worked so hard to weave.

SHORT STORY

GET UP AND CHRISTMAS AGAIN

BY ZARA MENHENNET

As you stand in the darkness, the snow reflects grey from the night sky. Houses line the village green and a little further along, the pub walls puff their cheeks against the bitter wind. Tucked inside, the revellers cheer the end of work over mulled wine and soggy Yorkshires, the Christmas season now upon them. Cars clutter the narrow streets that lead to the square where a dull lamp post stands at each corner, one flickering above the local Post Office, hidden inside the village shop.

It is here that we find our story, the tale that has been told in so many ways, the words repeated in fables, myths and by persistent school teachers - If you fall, get up and try again.If you follow me a moment, up this muddy path that goes behind the village shop, you'll see that we arrive at the old rectory. Long-time converted; it now houses a family who moved to the village several years ago, and like most, Christmas is very special.   It is a time where one over spends on everything, eats too much and if memory serves well, Christmas cards are sent out to all – even to those we never talk to.

Now, press your nose up against the window to the right side of the door - be careful of the window box - you can see into the living room which runs the width of the house. As you see, it's compact, or as the estate agent prefers to label it 'cosy'. To the left, a comfy three-seater couch is overladen with coloured throw cushions and beside it, a small wooden table houses the empty hot chocolate cups from earlier. Crayons and papers litter the centre table, while more pens disappear beneath the sofa, lost forever by the family cat.

If you look to the right, a chimney lights the room, and filling the corner on the far side is the most splendid tree. Decked with all the tinsel and Christmas balls the shop had for sale, the unbalanced décor can be accounted for by family effort. The shortest – or youngest you see, decorated the bottom while the adults had the privilege to place the star - if your nose is getting cold, you are too close to the glass, or if you've fogged it, take a step back - Can you see clearly? Now, look closely, for the story of 'never give up' starts here, in this very room…

Silver cap askew, his cheeks reflected the warmth of the chimney before him. Christmas lights flashing and mingling with green pine needles, he had dozed off as the TV repeated Mariah Carey for the umpteenth time that night. He had been reflecting back on life. How he had got to where he was, and how pleased he felt with his current position. For you see, not all of us find our purpose so quickly. For some, it is a lifetime's pursuit of dogged unhappiness that leads us nowhere. For others, at dawn's light we know our exact coordinates, and set out on life's shortcut to fulfil that clear ambition.

'Uncle,' called a voice in his subconscious, 'Uncle.'

Eyes opening, he peered beside him to see a small red face staring up at him. 'What is it?' he mumbled.

'Can you tell us, again?'

'Tell you what?'

'The story of how you got here! Please, Uncle. Tell it again!'

Smiling, he twisted slightly and yawning, he heaved a sigh. 'Well, you know, I didn't know I would end up here. Some call it destiny, others fate. For me, it was simply luck.'

By now, more had turned to listen to the Christmas classic that would be repeated many times.

'It all started the day I was made. I remember the blinding lights overhead as I rolled out, spanking new, a dull black round, ready to be dressed in my best for the festive season. Together with my companions, we travelled the many miles of conveyor belt before we divided, each destined for different colours. It was right then that I knew I was destined for the best. I was going to be gold! And what was more, glittery too.'

'And everybody loves gold, right Uncle,' chanted the little face.

'Exactly, and red too in the festive period. Just look where you are,' he winked. 'So young, and placed right beside me.' The red bauble blushed as the others looked her way.

'I remember it all so well,' he continued. 'There were thousands of us, and even though we were being shunted along at an alarming rate, I was able to get a glimpse at the blue and silver production lines. They were fewer in number than us, and appeared to be taking life at a much slower pace. But, before we reached the end, the lines merged once more. I was packaged with a lovely little red number from Production Line 23, a gorgeous one she was, destined she said, to be placed higher on the tree than I, as her "petite-ness" was designed for smaller branches.'

'Well, most years I am higher than you,' scowled the little red face. 'It just so happens that tree decorating is now a family event, so I don't get placed where I should.'

'True, but you are still as gorgeous as the day you were made. Look at me, my silver cap all askew,' he laughed. 'Even my thread that holds me here is wearing thin.'

'Enough already, get on with the story,' cut in another silver face higher up.'I'm new this year. What happened next?'

Eyes twinkling, Uncle continued. 'Black.Yes, black. That was all we saw for the next few months. There was no room to roll, and not a crack of light entered our box. We were so frightened as we felt the earth move beneath us, swelling and heaving its heavy breast. You see, we had been labelled for the UK, and not knowing it, had crossed the channel, all suffering with mal de mer. "YUK" would have been a better label for our box by the time we finished our trip. There was so much glitter at the bottom, that it's a wonder that we were even put up for sale!

But we were, and only in the best of them. You see, we were selected to go to Knightsbridge while our fellow companions were divided between ASDA and some local stores in Southampton. Oh, you should have seen it,' tears filled Uncle's eyes, 'the lights of Knightsbridge, I'll never forget.' He rubbed himself against the pine needles as he slipped into his own thoughts.

Silence fell in the room, the TV off and the embers burning. Beyond the window, the snow fell gracefully, filling the window box that sat beside the front door. Snoring now replaced the Christmas jingles as beneath a pile of blankets children slept on the sofa. Uncle watched as parents woke them gently to take them to bed, the cat toasting beside the dying fire.

'My family,' he sighed. 'They were my destiny. I sat upon the shelves at Knightsbridge for only two days before they bought me. I had been placed at eye-level, and the first to lift me from the shelf was a young woman dressed in torn jeans and a studded beanie. I shook in my box, dropping glitter everywhere. I knew my life would be shortened in her hands; I could feel it in my hollow shell.Next, a small boy ran with me through the store before abandoning me in the frozen food aisle! I shivered in my silver cap, before I was once more moved through to my own department, to only be dropped off in the Secret Santa Pick-n-Mix.'

'What happened?' squeaked a voice from further down the tree.

'Julie found me. She was only four years old then, but she saved me from the worst fate any Christmas bauble can face – sales. For me, she changed my destiny and that's how I wound up here upon her tree.'

'But why is your thread white and not silver like the others?' asked another voice.

Uncle shivered, his brilliance fading. 'That,' he whispered, 'is the material of nightmares.'

The tree trembled slightly, the first sign of movement that night. For even the pine needles quivered at the story they knew would be told. A fear so great, that few were able to re-tell it, to pass on the warning to other Christmas decorations. Silence.

'It was my first night on the tree,' whispered Uncle. 'I felt proud. I had been placed among the twinkling lights upon the most beautiful tree selected that morning. You see, my position was just a little higher than I am now, but beside the mantelpiece, the perfect place to be seen by all the living room and the outside world.'He stalled, his mind's eye flashing back to that night, a ripple of fear cursing up his thread.

'It's ok, Uncle. You don't have to tell it.'

'I must!' he shouted. 'Or I will never overcome this terror that lives with me when the lights go out.'
The red face fell silent.

'The family had gone to bed; the fire dim and we were left alone for the night. I remember looking out across the living room, I had seen something move in the darkness. A shape or a blur, I wasn't sure, but it was gone. I shook myself, knowing I was being silly, but then - wait!I saw something move again, this time near the sofa. It was getting closer, moving stealthily through the shadows towards us. I quivered; I couldn't help it! A black movement could be seen near the base of the fireplace, small, but quick. I looked to the living room door, but the family were asleep, unaware of the dangers that lay downstairs. My eyes looked to the fireplace once more, but it had gone.'

Up the tree, a little silver ball shuddered on its string. 'I don't want to know!' he cried. 'I'm scared!'

'So was I,' Uncle assured him. 'Where had it gone? My eyes looked about the room to no avail, when a feeling crossed my glittered being, a sensation that it was closer than before. I shut my eyes; I could feel the hot breath against my surrounding needles! I had to look. I had to know what was there beside me on the mantelpiece. Peeping, my eyes shot open, meeting with another set of amber green eyes with black slits. Its whiskers twitching, it leaned towards me. And then it happened, the last time I ever saw my silver thread. A paw smacked me sideways, throwing me into the air! I flew high, but landed softly amongst the branches of a fallen tree.'

The other baubles gasped, quivering in the caps. For each and every one of them knew that the same creature still resided in the house, waiting each year to do the same.

For you see, as I stated at the beginning, this is a story of 'If you fall, get up and try again', just like that golden Christmas bauble.

A FALL DAY IN MARYLAND USA

BY MADISON LIPSKY

One day its 80 degrees, the next it's a bitter 40. The manic episodes of our bipolar weather keep people on their feet, forcing them to live day by day. This uncertainty is somewhat exciting, but mostly it is frustrating. We must be careful of the trickery days in which the mornings are frosty, but the afternoons start to shine through with unpredictable heat. This is where layers come in handy, easy access to the removal of clothing, as well as the ability to put more warmth on if needed. The back road drives become a vision of loveliness as forests of thick trees and their dazzling changing leaves guide the driver's home. Long drives become the perfect occasion to listen to Fleet Wood Mac while sipping on a pumpkin flavored coffee with an extra shot of espresso. Allowing the roast of freshly brewed coffee to overshadow ones being with comforting heat, as if one's body never felt the chilly air that comes and goes from the outside winds. It makes getting where needed to be much faster, much more scenic, and much more appreciated. Certain scenic routes may make the driver ponder true love and its magical existence. The ocean waters off the coast become too cold to submerge one's body but it is still a beautiful sight to behold and to dance along the rim of the crashing tides is a joyful experience. Even though the weather is brisk with anticipation for family gatherings and holiday cheer we still eat as many crabs as we can before the unforgiving winter arrives, before our seafood stock surely declines, getting our last taste of Old Bay before its seasonal flavor goes into hibernation. We must say goodbye to the salty memorable taste of our ocean and its traditional gifts, at least until spring circles back around. People around charm city are draped in black and purple jerseys in celebration of purple Fridays and victory Mondays. Football is something we take very seriously as religion isn't the only thing that makes our Sundays sacred. Our pride in our bird city teams ultimately brings us closer together as a community, making the holidays that much more cheerful. Pumpkins become frequent decorations among the neighborhoods, being placed in temporary homes on people's porches and windowsills. Sometimes with the passing of Halloween people are so eager for the holidays that Christmas trees begin to shine through home windows no later than November first. The fleeting aromas of cinnamon, crisp leaves, cold air, burning wood, and pumpkin pie can be discovered anywhere, if one is fortunate enough to encounter such pleasant fall greetings. The bright colors of fall and its warming energy spread from the ocean waves to the city lights to the tops of each mountain, little America people might say as it is a fall day in Maryland USA.

A REGULAR AFTERNOON IN LONDON

BY SARA DOZAI

Sitting at a table in a London cafe, I looked at my surroundings. Everything was filled with people, a welcome change after the lonely year I've experienced due to COVID-19. While I was at the cafe alone, I didn't feel lonely. The people surrounding me energised me. They felt like a light shining in an otherwise quiet room. I took my copy of the New Yorker out of my crimson red bag and started reading. Usually, I read in parks because nature gives me a sense of peace and connection to the earth, however, today I decided to do it at a coffee place for a change. In the midst of my first article, I couldn't help but overhear a conversation two girls next to me were having. They weren't aware of me listening in, as they spoke German. They looked fully at ease and I understood them. When I speak Croatian in London, I feel like I'm speaking a secret language no one but my friends and I understand. However, that is not the case. While most people don't speak Croatian, there have been a few rather embarrassing encounters when other Croatian people passed by while me and my best friend were making the most absurd comment you could imagine. However, I digress. The girls were talking about the concept of feeling at ease with oneself. I wanted to stop listening, but I just couldn't. Something about their conversation intrigued me. Perhaps it was the intimacy between them that drew me in. Perhaps it was just my ever so curious mind or the instinct of a writer smelling a good story. I don't think I'll ever know for certain, but it doesn't even matter. The conversation started with the idea of getting a tattoo. A girl, whose name I do not know, and would conceal even if I did, described a white circle she was intending to tattoo just above her ankle. She saw the tattoo in a dream after doing yoga. The white ink would compliment her pale skin better than the black one. Perhaps this would make the tattoo barely visible, but that didn't matter. She wasn't getting the tattoo for the eyes of others. It was a need of her soul to know that it was there, as it represented her as a complete entity. The reason behind getting it was the desire to feel whole, even when immersed fully in a relationship with another. Just as the server came back with my tea, the pale-skinned girl changed the topic and went on to talk about love and relationships. Her friend with kind chocolate eyes full of understanding allowed her to revisit the topic as it was understood that this was not the first time they'd discussed it. The story she told was not unfamiliar to me. While I have never experienced it myself, many of my friends have. Her heart longed for a boy she used to hook up with and still talks to. He, on the other hand, does not wish for an exclusive relationship. Perhaps it is the lack of intense liking of the girl from his side, perhaps it is a fear of commitment. The only thing I know is that I've heard this story before, well, not exactly this one, but a variation on the theme. Then come the questions that consume the girl's mind. Why does he not want to be with me? Is he afraid of relationships? Am I not enough for him? Is it simply immaturity? A 20-year-old girl becomes a philosopher in the blink of an eye when love is involved. A million questions and a billion possibilities awaken in her mind. Then come the inevitable 3 AM talks with friends or even parents. Moms usually tell their daughters that the guys are just not on their level yet. Girlfriends call the guys assholes and complain about them. The conversations take a loop-like feeling and become automatic. The girl still dwells on the past, while the people around her are just repeating themselves on end. However, there comes a point, when the girl truly lets go and decides to close that chapter once and for all. While the pale-skinned girl was still not there, I felt a certainty in my heart that she was nearing that moment and I felt good about it. Experiences shape us into the people we are meant to become. Sometimes they are heart-wrecking, while other times they are extraordinarily beautiful. I don't deceive myself into thinking that I will ever see this girl again or that I will know how her life turns out. Nevertheless, this conversation affected me more than any of the two girls will ever know and I am grateful for that. A regular day at a cafe suddenly turned into a story-telling session that I will remember for at least a couple coming years.

Contact us

You can contact Hermes Magazine in these ways.

Email:
Hermesmagazinelondon@yahoo.com

Website:
www.hermesmagazine.yolasite.com

LinkedIn:
www.linkedin.com/company/hermesmagazine

Instagram:
www.instagram.com/hermesmagazinelondon